MW01518923

# Leading to Learn:
## Learning to Lead

Organizational Leadership for the Child Care
and Youth Development Director

# Leading to Learn:
## Learning to Lead

Organizational Leadership for the Child Care
and Youth Development Director

**Sparrow Media Group**
Farmington, Minnesota

# Leading to Learn: Learning to Lead

## Organizational Leadership for the Child Care and Youth Development Director

**Library of Congress Cataloging-in-Publication Data**
Ashcraft, Michael S., 1966-
  Leading to learn, learning to lead : organizational leadership for the child care and youth development director / Michael S. Ashcraft and Chelsea W. Ashcraft.
     p. cm.
  ISBN 978-0-9829526-1-0 (pbk.)
  1.  Child care services--Administration. 2.  School-age child care. 3.  Youth development. 4.  Leadership.  I. Ashcraft, Chelsea W., 1970- II. Title.
  HQ778.5.A84 2011
  362.71'20684--dc22

                    2011011239

Printed and bound in the United States.
Quantity discounts are available for organizations or universities.

Contact:
Sparrow Media Group
16588 Fieldcrest Avenue
Farmington, MN 55024
www.sparrowmediagroup.com

*Leadership and learning are indispensable to each other.*
*—John F. Kennedy*

*To believe in a child is to believe in the future. Through their aspirations they will save the world. With their combined knowledge, the turbulent sea of hate and injustice will be calmed. They will champion the causes of life's underdogs, forging a society without class discrimination. They will supply humanity with music and beauty, as it has never known. They will endure. Towards these ends, I pledge my life's work. I will supply the children with tools and knowledge to overcome the obstacles. I will pass on the wisdom of my years and temper it with patience. I shall impact in each child the desire to fulfill his or her dream.*
*—Henry James*

# Acknowledgements

*In all things acknowledge Him and He will direct thy path.*
—*King Solomon, Proverbs 3:6*

We are grateful for our colleagues at Children's Choice Child Care Services, Inc., which has been our learning laboratory for the past twelve years. We are grateful for their enthusiasm and commitment to their jobs and for teaching us how to lead.

We give special acknowledgement to Dr. Rich Allen, our extraordinary teacher, who taught us how to teach. By applying his instruction, we have transformed our staff training events and keynotes into exceptional learning experiences. His influence can be seen in this book in our use of frames, stories, illustrations, and music. For more information visit www.greenlighteducation.net.

We have learned everything we know from others. This book is based on the research of others, although we have attempted to lead you through what we have learned in a creative way. We are fortunate to drink from the wells that others have dug, so we acknowledge the great statesmen—from theorists, researchers, teachers, and writers to our own parents and grandparents. The well diggers we have learned directly from include: Jim Ollhoff, Laurie Ollhoff, Fred Bartling, Rich Allen, Eric Jensen, Mickey Selligson, Ellen Gannet, Tracey Ballas, Susan O'Connor, Liz Joye, Jim Cain, Michael Brandwein, Bob Ditter, Sandy Luck, and many others.

## Is this book for me?

The primary target audience of this book includes leaders of early childhood, child care, and youth development organizations. The authors are executive directors of a not-for-profit school-age child care organization, so many of the stories and examples come out of the afterschool world. Leaders in the fields of Early Childhood Education, Middle (School-Age) Childhood Education, Camps, Afterschool Enrichment Programs, and Afterschool Recreation Programs will also find strong applications to their work.

This book is relevant for leaders working in community centers, charter schools, and many human service professions.

The leadership philosophy presented here is modern, effective, and powerful for leaders in any field.

## Why the book?

Let us begin by first describing who we are not and what this book is not. We are not larger-than-life, alluring, charismatic leaders who motivate and exhort our followers through our mere presence in the room. We are not geniuses; not know-it-all experts who have learned everything there is to learn about leadership. You will never see either of us on the cover of Time magazine. We are not great and powerful sages on the center stage of our organization. We are not compelling, fascinating, high-profile bosses with hundreds of helpers. This book is not a recipe for charismatic leadership. This book will not help you to become any of the things we describe in this paragraph.

We are not show dogs; we are working dogs. And we are lucky. We were fortunate enough to have some lousy bosses, so we learned what not to do and what not to be. We were fortunate enough to have some great bosses, so we learned some great skills also.

We founded Children's Choice Child Care Services, Inc., based in Albuquerque, New Mexico. We were lucky enough to create our own organization, and have enjoyed the privilege of having the power to send ourselves "to school" in many ways. This organization has been an enriching and educational institution for us. It has been our school of leadership—a leadership laboratory. We've made mistakes, learned from them, and are bound to make many more. We sent ourselves "to school" through many conferences, workshops, and seminars. We have hired many of the greatest minds in our profession to come and work directly with our colleagues and ourselves. We were lucky enough to send ourselves to formal school as well. Chelsea earned a master's degree in early childhood education and administration. Mike earned a master's degree in school-age child care and is at the "all-but-dissertation" stage with his doctorate of education degree in organizational leadership. We have been sponges for learning, and consider it our jobs to be the lead learners in our organization. We have been on a mission of learning how to lead. We never stop trying to learn; never stop trying to be qualified for the jobs we are lucky enough to have.

Our organization has been very successful. We have experienced steady growth. We have a strong reputation for quality in our community. One of our programs was the first in the country to receive national accreditation after the initial pilot project. We provide the only accredited school-based programs in the state. We paved the way for other school-age programs to be licensed. We have low staff turnover and high staff morale and commitment. We have children who used to attend our programs come back and seek employment with us as young adults. These former participants tell us that they learned so much and had such a great time with us that they want to give this to the children of today. When we think about the reasons for our achievements, we know that we owe our success to the phenomenal people we are privileged to work with and learn with at our organization.

We all care deeply about our work. We are never satisfied with our current level of quality and success. We all have an intense will to continuously improve for our colleagues, stakeholders, children, and families. We will never consider our organization to be good enough. We are all passionate about making our programs great!

We have been very fortunate and we are obligated and privileged to share what we have learned. Part of our mission is to share what we do and what we have learned with others. We began our work of leading others to learn when the New Mexico State Department of Education contracted with us to research "best practices" in school-age child care programming and to provide training and technical assistance to impoverished programs in New Mexico. This research led to the publication of our books, *Best Practices: Guidelines for School-Age Programs and the Best Practices Workbook.*

As we taught, we learned. We have been fortunate enough to share what we have learned with thousands of practitioners all across the country. We've also been accreditation endorsers for the National Afterschool Association. Through this experience we've been invited into many programs to observe and rate them on established quality standards. We've observed and consulted with many Air Force, Army, and civilian programs.

We've been lucky enough to provide training, technical assistance, and consulting with many diverse types of afterschool programs: academic based, recreation based, publicly funded, privately funded, fee based. We've observed many effective and ineffective leadership strategies. We've worked with a few lousy organizations, many good organizations, and some great organizations. In every example, the difference between lousy, good, and great is the leadership.

In our profession, when someone is good at working with children they are promoted away from them—promoted behind a desk into a leadership position. Often they receive no formal training or education in leadership. All of our experience and research has led us to the inescapable conclusion that leadership is vital, fundamental, paramount—the overriding, absolute key to success. We have discovered that leadership is absolutely a learnable skill. We have also noted a lack of tools and information to help those who are great with children learn to be great with their adult colleagues.

The purpose of this book is to help those who are good with kids become great leaders of the organizations that serve them. Leadership is all about learning. Leadership and learning are indispensable to each other. Leadership is not a genetic trait. There have been a few charismatic leaders throughout history who seem to have been born with alluring and compelling leadership traits—big personalities who make headlines and become celebrities. But there are many more authentic leaders who lack pretense, who are quiet, reserved, socially awkward, and even shy, but have a fierce resolve for doing what is in the best interest of staff, children, and families. They have faith in people and the determination and will to improve and learn. The type of leadership we need in this profession IS learnable. Leaders are not born—they make themselves. They learn to lead, and they lead others to help them learn—they create more leaders.

When we are old and retired we want to be able to look back at our professional lives and our wonderful organization that impacted others in the U.S. and beyond, that developed children, created confident caring leaders, healthier kids, healthier families, and healthier communities—an organization that positively influenced the world—and proudly say, "Wow, we used to work there!" We hope that you truly enjoy and benefit from *Leading to Learn: Learning to Lead.*

# Contents

## Chapter 3: Playing the Part

## Part III: The Meat
## Chapter 4: Practicing the Art

## Chapter 5: Learning for Life

## Chapter 6: Giving Super Powers

## Part IV: The Details
### Chapter 7: Influencing the Individuals

### Chapter 8: Making Variety Stew

## Chapter 9: Tackling Turnover

## Chapter 10: Making the Most of Meetings

## Part V: The End
## Chapter 11: Wrapping it Up

# Part I: The Beginning

## Read This: Navigating this Book

*There are quotes introducing each chapter and many subjects. Some are wise. Some are thought provoking. Some are silly. Some are just plain weird.*
*—Mike Ashcraft*

*I quote others to better express myself.*
*—Michael de Montaigne*

*I hate quotations.*
*—Ralph Waldo Emerson*

*Let the good times roll!*
*—B. B. King*

There are recurring headings and little elements in every chapter of this book. We thought a description of these might help you to use this book.

## Story Time

Stories have been used throughout the course of human history to convey knowledge and deep truths, and preserve records of the past. Stories engage emotions, imagination, and the auditory and visual centers of the brain. We use many metaphors and personal stories throughout this book to inspire and to teach.

In telling our personal stories we had to decide on a writing convention to use that identified which of the two authors was telling the story. We could use "One of the authors experienced…" We could refer to ourselves specifically using the third person: "Mike was standing on a mountain, and…" We could use a phrase like, "When I was a girl…" leaving you to realize that it is Chelsea telling the story. We decided that whenever we go into storytelling mode to identify the storyteller in the third person and then switch over to a more natural first person voice. "Chelsea learned an important lesson about leadership. Here is her story. When I first became a supervisor…"

Some of the more obvious stories, metaphors, and fables are labeled as "Story Time." Some of them speak directly to the point being explored in that section of the book, some tie the point back to child development leadership, and some are feel-good, inspiring stories about life.

We have collected and written many of these stories to use in our training events. We have gathered many from attending the training events of others. In the tradition of storytelling, we hear stories, make them our own and retell them in our own way. We have modified many we heard elsewhere to make points needed for this book. Dr. Rich Allen (see acknowledgements) shared some of the stories in this book with us in the spirit of passing on knowledge. We pass all of these stories along to you in the same spirit.

## Bringing It Home
In our concluding remarks for each chapter we will bring it all home for you. Throughout this book we make links between the theory, information, or research presented and your day-to-day work life, but in these sections we will reflect on the big picture of the chapter and how it applies to your child development leadership world. These sections are designed to help you apply the broader meaning of the knowledge to your "real life" context.

## Helpful Resources
There are hundreds of resources and references in this book. In these sections we highlight especially helpful resources to complement the content of each chapter. We draw attention to interesting and useful online information and experiences. We emphasize books that are "must reads" for the topic being explored.

## Try This
In these sections, we provide practical ideas you can use to explore and practice the information and skills discussed in each chapter. We include some things you can do with your staff team at work and things you can do on your own. We provide "real life" examples of steps you can take to implement the knowledge being shared in order to improve your leadership skills and success.

## Discussion Questions

Here we provide thought-provoking questions designed to help you apply the information to your mental models and your day-to-day practices. We designed questions that you can use in staff training to teach the concepts contained in this book.

# Part II: The Basics

## Chapter 1: Charting the Course

*Anyone can steer the ship, but it takes a real leader to chart the course.*
*—George Barna*

*Begin with the End in Mind.*
*—Stephen Covey*

*The future's so bright, I gotta wear shades.*
*—Timbuk 3*

### Introduction

*The very essence of leadership is that you have to have a vision. It's got to be a vision you articulate clearly and forcefully on every occasion. You can't blow an uncertain trumpet.*
*—Reverend Theodore M. Hesburgh*

*If you want to move people, it has to be toward a vision that's positive for them, that taps important values, that gets them something they desire, and it has to be presented in a compelling way. That way, they feel inspired to follow.*
*—Martin Luther King, Jr.*

*A leader is one who knows the way, goes the way, and shows the way.*
*—John C. Maxwell*

Imagine your life is over. It's your funeral. Your friends, family, and colleagues are gathered there. They are speaking about you. A reporter is there to record it all and write a story about your life. What do you want them to say? You create what they will say in your actions today. Begin with the end in mind.

By definition leaders must know where they are going if they hope to lead. Leaders who don't know in which direction to go succeed only in leading people down an aimless and meaningless path. Developing a vivid picture of the future is an important part of creating a future that is better than today. Having a clear, motivating image of a desired future provides meaning and context to daily tasks. Focusing on a vision for the future can inspire people to reach higher and overcome challenges. Once created, a vision will help to structure decision making and policy setting in an organization.

Visioning is a common and effective strategy proven useful in many endeavors. Olympic athletes visualize themselves performing their specific feats, and this visualization is effective in helping them to perform better. Albert Einstein imagined himself traveling through the universe as a "man in a box" on a ray of light. This vision helped him develop the theory of general relativity.

Chelsea has a story about visioning. Here is her story. When I was a girl I did not like water. I never have; I still don't. Needless to say, I had a really hard time as a child in my swimming lessons. My parents paid for private swim lessons for one summer when I was eleven. Every day I struggled with the breaststroke. I was uncomfortable and scared so I was not very successful. One night, as I was dreading the next morning's lesson, I pictured myself doing the breaststroke. I pictured how it felt, what my arms and legs were doing, how I was breathing. It was very vivid in my mind; so vivid I still remember it today. When I got to my lesson the next day I miraculously did the breaststroke! Visioning is powerful.

Future-focused thinking is the one attribute that a leader must possess to create and shape an "intentional organization." An intentional organization is purposeful, created and led with a specific goal in mind. An intentional organization is grounded in specific objectives and it has a plan of action designed to accomplish these objectives. The culture of an intentional organization reflects a deliberate focus on a specific end result. In order for the organization to be purposeful, goal oriented, grounded in specific objectives, and focused on an end result, the leader must be able to see and articulate a vision—to chart a course for the future.

This essential leadership trait, which we call future-focused thinking, but which has been described in many ways, is a prevalent leadership attribute in research studies. Three out of four respondents in a research study selected the ability to look ahead as one of their most sought-after leadership traits (Kouzes & Posner, 1995). Peter Drucker calls this ability "managing for the future." Having a picture of where you are going is vital to leading and to getting your people and your organization where you want them to go.

A good vision is ideological, but possible; challenging, but realistic. It is not a wishful fantasy, but an attainable picture of the future. A good vision should be imaginable, desirable, feasible, focused, flexible, and communicable. A good vision portrays a picture of the future with some implicit or explicit commentary on why people should strive to create that future (Kotter, 1996). A vision can be a mental picture of the "ideal" organization, community, or youth program. Studies have shown that people are more likely to reach a goal if they can envision it and can imagine the steps to reach it.

Clarity of purpose and direction, and the ability to envision the future are paramount to effective leadership. Whether we call this a vision, a dream, a calling, a goal, or a personal agenda, the message is clear: leaders must know where they're going if they expect others to willingly join them on the journey. "Vision is the magnetic north that provides others with the capacity to chart their course toward the future" (Kouzes & Posner, 1995).

## Story Time: Dad's Toolbox

When Mike was a boy his dad had a toolbox. It wasn't like the cheap plastic ones they make these days. It was a big ole honkin' thing. I don't know how heavy it really was, but it was too heavy for me to lift it by myself.

One day my dad said to my brother and me, "Boys, get the toolbox and meet me on the roof. We're going to change your broken window screen." Our bedroom window opened up on the first floor roof. We had to access it by climbing up a fence with a thorny rose bush growing in it while carrying this behemoth of a toolbox. We lugged it up there and dragged it over to my dad and he held out his hand like a surgeon expecting a scalpel and said, "Screwdriver."

I said, "Which kind, Phillips or flat?" Dad said, "Doesn't matter." He inserted the screwdriver into the eye of the eye screw that attached the screen. He twisted the screwdriver in a circle with his index finger, quickly unscrewing the eye screw. He did this with all four screws and removed the old screen. He held up the new screen, saw that the holes lined up, and again said, "Screwdriver." He quickly replaced the eye screws, dusted his hands and said, "Hmm...that's it."

I said, "Dad, if that's all you needed, WHY did we have to bring this whole toolbox up here?" He said, "Boys, the more tools you have the more options you have to solve problems. You never know what you're going to see when you get into a job. Things are sometimes a lot more complex than they appear. If you have lots of tools and you have ALL of your tools with you when you go to a job, you'll be prepared to deal with whatever happens."

This is a good metaphor for what can happen in leadership situations. Things are sometimes very complex. It is in your best interest to add as many leadership tools to your tool belt as you can, and learn how to pick the right tool for the job. The purpose of this book is to give you many leadership tools with many practical ideas of how to use these tools to construct a dynamic, inclusive, high-performing, high-involvement organization.

## Learning and the Future
*The leader has to be practical and a realist, yet must talk the language of the visionary and the idealist.*
*—Eric Hoffer*

Future-focused thinkers must be voracious learners. Historians estimate that the core of knowledge is doubling every two years. New technologies are emerging monthly. In this "Information Age," leaders and employees can never be finished learning (Schwahn & Spady, 1998).

Future-focused leaders embrace new learning and change as a means to progress toward the way they want the organization to feel, to look, and to be in the future. They create useful learning experiences and provide clear and compelling opportunities for everyone to benefit from what they learn. They think about how the future is evolving and how that will affect the members of the organization.

To be an effective leader, you must be a hungry and perpetual learner, studying journal articles and newspaper reports, reading books, taking courses, and scanning the culture and the people around you for signs of the new and previously unrecognized (Farren & Kaye, 1996).

Future-focused thinkers must be insatiable lifelong learners that consider the learning process to be active, not passive. They must embrace the acquisition of insight and knowledge, and hold dear the views of potential futures as well as those of the present and the past, all being elements of continuous improvement. Future-focused leaders do not view the present as something outside of their own control, something to adapt to or react to, but rather as a reality of their own making. This perspective empowers them to take an active role in creating the future. Through paradigm-breaking imagination and innovation, they learn new things and align new systems in order to produce the world they live in and the future world that is to come.

Taking an active role in creating the future, not merely reacting or adapting to current situations, is easier said than done. Leaders must first be able to do this in their own lives. Thinking outside the box, not accepting others' decisions when they don't make sense, and challenging current views and beliefs are good first steps.

## Try This: Visionary Exercises
Try out one of the following exercises:
- Envision an article written in the future about you or your organization.
- Record your desired future in a diagram, sketch, model, or in a photographic montage.
- Imagine yourself receiving an award for a major accomplishment. What is the award for? What did you accomplish?
- Think about an ideal early childhood or afterschool program. What does it look like, sound like, feel like, and smell like? Make a list of the things that are already in place in your programs. Identify relatively easy, inexpensive actions you can take to improve quality. Create a plan for how you will need to tackle bigger changes.

- Politely question policies and procedures that don't make sense to you. Ask why they are in place and learn about the problem they are supposed to solve. Now try to think of better solutions to these problems.
- Argue your opposite belief about an article or current event with a friend. Work hard at making good, sound points. This helps you to understand others' perspectives better in the work situation.

## Bringing It Home

*Leadership is lifting a person's vision to high sights, the raising of a person's performance to a higher standard, the building of a personality beyond its normal limitations.*
*—Peter F. Drucker*

Let's bring this vision discussion home to the larger community of the child care profession. The visioning process must not only study and articulate desired outcomes for you personally and for your organization, but also be future-focused on what is happening in the field. Child care and youth development practitioners must be able to forecast trends in their organizations and in the profession. How will the relationships between state and federal departments of education and children, youth, and family departments change in the future? How will the increasing focus on academic achievement as reflected in standardized achievement tests affect the future of school-age care programs? Will the schools take over the delivery of early childhood, pre-k, and afterschool programs in order to access funding and out of pressure to improve test scores?

Visionary leaders and strategic thinkers in the field of child care and youth development must spend time studying the future: the applicant pool, the current workforce, trends in the profession, the professionalization of the field, staff turnover, job satisfaction, professional development, and the career lattice structure must be studied and engineered with the future in mind. Child care and youth development practitioners must develop core competencies consistent with the goals and values of the profession. Future-focused pre-service training requirements and continuing professional development frameworks that include in-service training, credential and certificate programs, and advanced degree programs must be created. As the competencies of caregivers increase, so must their compensation.

Worthy wages are important to the future of child care and youth development. Licensing of individual practitioners in addition to the licensing of school-age care organizations is inevitable. Visionary leaders must decide how this becomes reality.

Public awareness about the significance and importance of this field is on the rise. Child care and youth development practitioners must strategically influence public perception. Practitioners within the field must articulate the values and research-based best practices to those outside the profession.

Partnerships must be formed with allied professions such as juvenile justice, early childhood education, elementary education, health organizations, workforce development organizations, and other out-of-school-time organizations. Knowledge and understanding about the profession of afterschool and early childhood education must grow out of the increased public awareness and into a public mandate. The public must be advocates of the importance of early childhood education, school-age child care, and youth development programs to the entire education system. All of this will happen out of an understanding of a vision for our profession: healthier children, healthier families, and healthier communities.

## Envisioning a Vision

When visioning about the field of school-age care and child development, and about a single school-age care organization, the first questions to ask concern core beliefs and values. School-age practitioners must use a values-based framework and a code of ethics to guide them in visioning and strategic planning. What are your beliefs and values; the values of the field and of your individual organization?

For example, in our organization, we believe that quality school-age care is more than a safe place for kids to be while their parents are working, and it is more than a fun place to be. It is one of the few times in a child's day that provides the opportunity to interact positively with children of different ages. It is perhaps the only time in a day that teachers have the time to give significant one-on-one attention to individual children. We have the unique ability to teach the social skills that are essential in youth development, delinquency prevention, and the development of the future citizens of this country. We believe that we can join in true partnership with the family and the school in the role of participating in the positive development and education of our children.

In our organization, we value all of the people that make our organization strong, so we treat them as professionals, pay them competitively, invest in their training and professional development, treat them with caring and respect, help them to build their competencies, and trust them to act in the best interest of children and of our organization. We value long-term, big-picture, out-of-the-box thinking, so we look deeply into complex interrelationships, invest in wise decision making and problem solving, and give knowledge, information, power, and control to all of our staff. We value lifelong learning, so children and all staff members are encouraged to learn through their experiences. We value quality, so we exceed quality standards and provide a place for nurturing and the development of life skills. We value our children and our families, so we facilitate positive child development, workforce development, and societal contribution. We value ethical standards, so we facilitate honesty, fairness, respect, responsibility, trustworthiness, citizenship, and caring.

Our beliefs and values helped us to create our mission statement. "Children's Choice Child Care Services, Inc. is dedicated to facilitating the positive development of children by developing and maintaining school-age care programs that are a model of quality care—programs where children play, learn, grow, and make friends—programs where children are nurtured and develop life skills. Children's Choice will use these programs as a source of training and technical assistance for the larger community of school-age care practitioners."

The beliefs, values, and mission of Children's Choice all come together as the articulation of a vision. The vision is ideological, but possible. It is challenging, but realistic. It is not a wishful fantasy, but an attainable picture of our future. It is the end result of accomplishing our goals and our mission.

The vision of Children's Choice is that of a wonderful place filled with an extended family in true partnership with schools and families. It is a community that nurtures and truly cares for children, staff, and families. It is a mini-society that challenges children, staff, and families to be their best. It is a place where children, staff, and families learn and develop life skills. It is a place that "makes easier" the positive development and education of children. The vision of Children's Choice is to see healthier children, healthier families, and a healthier community.

## Try This: State Your Vision

*A man without character is like a ship without a rudder.*
*—Karl Maeser*

Go ahead, visualize your ideal life. Describe it. Create statements of beliefs and values, a mission statement for yourself personally, for your program, or for your organization. Use this to help you create a broad vision statement. If it sounds like motherhood and apple pie and is somewhat embarrassing, you are on the right track (Schwahn & Spady, 1998).

## Try This: Mind Mapping

Mind mapping is a type of graphic organizer; a powerful technique that can help in developing a vision or strategy, or expand thinking on a subject. The "map" uses words, ideas, lines, colors, pictures, and links to draw out associations and stimulate thinking. The technique works as well in large group brainstorming sessions as it does one-on-one with a coach.

While there are many different "mind mapping" systems, the basic process involves expanding on ideas using key words and branches. The objective is to make a complex topic easier to understand, explore, or remember. A mind map is a diagram used to represent words, ideas, tasks, or other items linked to and arranged around a central key word or idea. It is used to generate, visualize, structure, and classify ideas, and as an aid in study, organization, problem solving, decision making, and writing. Individuals can use mind mapping to sketch out a presentation, a paper, an event, or anything that needs to be organized into a series of thoughts and actions.

The advantages of using a mind map as a group brainstorming activity are:

- A group can work on it together-and all can be engaged;
- It provokes discussion;
- It can continually change;
- Participants can add/delete/link items;
- Pieces can be treated as individual mind maps;
- It is very visual, which appeals to visual learners.

Play with these simple mind maps:

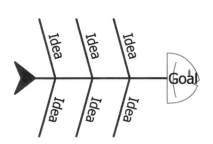

**The Fishbone**

With the Fishbone organizer, we begin with a goal or a big idea that we write in the head. Then we write ideas about how to accomplish the goal or project on the ribs. These might be the tasks or objectives we agree on that support our goal. For example, if our goal is to increase parent participation, then ideas might include: holding a family picnic, creating a suggestion box, surveying parents about their ideas, having a talent show with the kids, explaining the intentionality of your methods in the parent newsletter, etc.

The ideas then may branch off horizontally. For example, one person suggests creating a Facebook page for families; another person immediately suggests a Twitter page, then updates to the Web site, then YouTube videos, then electronic newsletters, etc.—a whole fish rib becomes dedicated to strategic ways to use technology to support our goal.

**The Spider Web**

We use the Spider Web most often for guided brainstorming. We draw a circle in the middle of a blank sheet of paper and write a project, goal, dream, values, or idea in the center of the circle. In our example we used our belief in the importance of playfulness. Then we drew spokes or branches radiating out from the central circle, each providing a place for brainstorming about subtopics such as a playful staff, playful environment, and purposeful play. Then we added more spokes radiating outward each developing the idea more completely. This is a little like that energizer bunny—it just keeps going and going and going.

## Conclusion

*Vision without action is merely a dream.*
*—Joel Barker*

*Leadership is the capacity to translate vision into reality.*
*—Warren G. Bennis*

While focusing on the future, leaders should not neglect the past or the present. The adage "hindsight is twenty-twenty" illustrates the importance of the past. The past gives us a history of knowledge and experience from which to illuminate our view of the present and the future. Understanding, deliberating, and reflecting on the past enhances our ability to be future-focused. The best visionary, future-focused leaders are those with the longest time horizons—those who understand their past (Kouzes & Posner, 1995). We learn a lot by studying the past, but the present gives us the opportunity to apply what we have learned. The opportunity to shape the future exists in the present.

Being future-focused doesn't mean having the awesome powers of a prophet or the abilities of a clairvoyant, but rather to have a clear picture of a preferred future toward which the organization should steer. While not mystical and magical, future-focused thinkers can be visionary leaders. Visionary future-focused leaders look far beyond the tried and true. They develop the compass reading on which to chart their course—a course organizations depend upon in a world of constant change. They establish the concrete, innovative direction of where their organizations must go and how they must operate to meet the changing and escalating needs and expectations of their customers (Schwahn & Spady, 1998). Envisioning your dream is the first step. Next we'll discuss how to get to work and make your dream a reality!

## Discussion Questions

1. Think about your personal life. Do you feel in control and make decisions to guide your future, or do you react and adapt to life's problems? Make a list of decisions you have made that were proactive and decisions or actions you took that were reactive.

2. Think about your perspective toward issues and problems. Do you say things like, "The bus left without me" (I have no control) or do you say things like, "I didn't organize my time well enough to make it to the bus stop on time" (I have personal control and responsibility)?

3. If you looked into a crystal ball, what would your organization, program, or community look like in ten years?

4. Are you focused on the right questions? Take a moment and reflect what you spend your time thinking about when it comes to the future of your organization and the role you play.

5. Do you see yourself as a future-focused visionary leader? Are you satisfied with the state of your organization and the state of the profession? If not, what differences would you like to see? What is an ideal future?

## Helpful Resources

Get help with and tips for creating your vision statement at
www.mindtools.com/pages/article/newLDR_90.htm
And at
www.timethoughts.com/goalsetting/vision-statements.htm

Tony Buzan is the originator of mind mapping. His Web site is
www.buzanworld.com

For easy to learn and use mind mapping software for visualizing, organizing, and brainstorming, visit
www.mindmapper.com

## Reference Notes

Farren, C., & Kaye, B. (1996). New skills for new leadership roles. In Hesselbein, F., Goldsmith, M., & Beckhard, R. (Eds.). *The leader of the future.* San Francisco: Jossey-Bass Publishers.

Kotter, J. (1996). *Leading Change.* Boston: Harvard Business School Press.

Kouzes, J. & Posner, B. (1995). *The leadership challenge: How to keep getting extraordinary things done in organizations.* San Francisco: Jossey-Bass, Inc.

Morgan, G. (1997). *Images of Organization.* Thousand Oaks, CA: Sage Publications, Inc.

Morris, L. (1995). Development strategies for the knowledge era. In Chawla, S., & Renesch, J. (Eds.), *Learning Organizations* (p. 335). Portland, OR: Productivity Press.

Schwahn, C. & Spady, W. (1998). *Total leaders: Applying the best future-focused change strategies to education.* Arlington, VA: American Association of School Administrators. San Francisco, CA: Jossey-Bass Publishers.

# Chapter 2: Pouring Foundations

*The loftier the building, the deeper must the foundation be laid.*
—*Thomas à Kempis*

*A wise man…built his house upon the rock; and the rain fell, and the floods came; and the winds blew and beat against that house, but it did not fall because it had been founded on the rock…a foolish man…build his house upon the sand;…and it fell, and great was the fall of it.*
—*Matthew 6:24–27 (RSV)*

*Don't know much about history.*
—*Sam Cooke*

## Introduction
*Build your empire on the firm foundation of the fundamentals.*
—*Lou Holtz*

We ended our discussion of visionary, future-focused leaders by pointing out the importance of understanding the past. Leaders can most effectively chart a course into the future when they understand the lessons of history. Exploring the past gives us the knowledge from which to illuminate our perception of the present and the future. Understanding, deliberating, and reflecting on our past enhances our ability to be future-focused. By studying the history of your organization, your profession, your community, and of leadership theory and research, you can understand where momentum and leverage exists and you can most effectively chart a course into a future that is great for yourself and your organization.

The following is a history of some of the major schools of thought on management and leadership and on organizational ethics. It is a description of some of the most significant theorists and their contributions to the study of leadership. These are various theories based on beliefs regarding people, their capacity for thinking, their motivation, and their potential. This story begins with Frederick Taylor's Scientific Management Theory at the turn of the twentieth century, and it ends with W. Edwards Deming's Total Quality Management

Theory. While by no means conclusive, the theories we chose to include show widely different thoughts and ideas on management techniques. It is our hope that this chapter provides you with a foundation upon which to begin building your personal leadership theory base.

## Story Time: Professional or Processional?

Processionary caterpillars feed on pine needles. They move in an undulating parade-like fashion across tree limbs, one after another, each connected to the tail of the preceding caterpillar. Jean-Henry Fabri, a renowned French naturalist, decided to experiment with a group of these caterpillars. Patiently enticing them to the rim of a large flowerpot, he connected the first caterpillar to the last, forming a fuzzy circular cavalcade with no beginning and no end. He expected the insects to eventually catch on to the joke, tire of the endless march, and start off in some new direction. But no. Through sheer force of habit, they circled the rim of the pot for seven days and seven nights.

An ample supply of food was close at hand and plainly visible, but it was outside the range of the caterpillars' self-imposed limits. Realizing the creatures would not stop or redirect themselves, even if faced with starvation, Jean-Henry gently broke the chain and led the hungry procession to nearby food and water.

Sometimes we, as child care and youth development professionals or as leaders, do the things we do just because we have always done them that way. We go through the motions. Sometimes we practice our craft the same way we have always done it, and then are surprised to get the same results time after time. Isn't this the definition of insanity?

There are two important morals to this story. First, professionals and leaders develop their own styles and their own philosophies, but unlike processionary caterpillars, these philosophies are built upon a strong theory base. In child care, program philosophies must be built upon a theory base of child development. In leadership, management and organizational philosophies must be based on a theory base of leadership. Effective leaders engage in behaviors that are intentional.

Second, professional leaders must be "critically reflective practitioners." Their theory base is constantly being improved. They engage in behaviors grounded in their theory base, while using real-life experience to improve and expand their theory base. They create systems of learning where they continuously improve both their theory base and their practices through endless learning cycles. So, don't mindlessly go with the flow of the status quo. Take action based on your personal growing leadership theory base.

## Scientific Management Theory

At the turn of the century, the most notable organizations were large and industrialized. Often they included ongoing, routine tasks that manufactured a variety of products. The United States highly prized scientific and technical matters, including careful measurement and specification of activities and results. Management tended to do the same.

Frederick Taylor developed the Scientific Management Theory, popular from 1890–1940. He was an American engineer who became one of the most influential organizational theorists of the twentieth century. Taylor's Scientific Management Theory emphasized the efficient division of labor into small, specialized, standardized jobs that were carefully matched to the capacities of workers. It espoused careful specification and measurement of all organizational tasks. Tasks were standardized as much as possible. Workers were rewarded and punished (Osland, Kolb, & Rubin, 2001).

He advocated five simple principles:
1. Shift all responsibility and thinking to the managers.
2. Use scientific methods to determine the one best way of doing a job, and designate tasks accordingly.
3. Select the best person to perform each job.
4. Train the worker to perform the job efficiently.
5. Monitor worker performance to ensure that appropriate work procedures are followed and that results are achieved (Morgan, 1997).

This approach appeared to work well for organizations with assembly lines and other mechanistic, routinized activities. Taylor's ideal manager scientifically determined the organizational goals, divided the work up between employees in a scientifically efficient manner, trained and monitored employees to accomplish specific tasks, and rewarded them with wage incentives.

However, Taylor gained a reputation as a major enemy of the workingman in his view of organizations as machines and the employees as automatons. He emphasized cooperation between the managers who did all of the thinking and organizing (the "brains") and the workers who implemented their instructions (the "hands"). Taylor was fond of telling his workers, "You are not supposed to think. There are other people paid for thinking around here" (Morgan, 1997).

## Administrative Theory and Mechanistic Organizations

Administrative/Bureaucratic Theory and the metaphor of organizations as machines arose out of the Industrial Revolution, when it was shown that many things could be assembled from piles of interchangeable parts. At this point in history (1930–1950), managers were struggling with the increasing troubles and tribulations of larger and larger organizations. This theory is grounded in the metaphor of the organization as a machine. In Mechanistic Organizations, all tasks were rigidly defined and broken down into specialized distinct parts. Authority and control were centralized within a clear, vertical chain of communication and command, and there was a high level of formalization, rigid departmentalization, and a narrow span of control. Mechanistic Organizations were rigid bureaucracies with strict rules, narrowly defined tasks, top-down communication, and centralized decision making (Osland, et al, 2001).

One major contribution to this theory was made by German sociologist Max Weber, who observed many parallels between the mechanization of industry and the increase of bureaucratic forms of organization. He embellished the Scientific Management Theory with his Administrative/Bureaucratic Theory. Weber focused on dividing organizations into hierarchies, establishing strong lines of authority and control. He suggested organizations develop comprehensive and detailed standard operating procedures for all routinized tasks.

He believed in an ideal bureaucracy as a form of organization that emphasized exactness, speed, precision, regularity, reliability, and especially efficiency through the creation of a fixed division of tasks, hierarchical supervision, rules, and regulations (Morgan, 1997). In those days, bureaucracy did not have the negative connotations it does today. Bureaucracy was a good thing. It improved consistency and fairness. It was a solution to the nepotism, favoritism, and unprofessional behavior found in organizations of that time (Osland, et al, 2001).

When an engineer designs a machine, the task is to define a network of parts, each with their own specific function that will function in sequence to accomplish some work. Classical theorists wanted to achieve a similar design function in organizations. Henri Fayol (France), F. W. Mooney (U.S.), and Col. Lyndell Urwick (England) advocated the study of management as a discipline. They believed that ideal managers are planners, organizers, coordinators, organizers, and controllers and commanders (Morgan, 1997; Osland, et al, 2001). Theoretically, if the ideal manager designed the organization correctly and followed established principles of management, the organization would succeed.

This type of organizational structure is most effective for performance based on routine behaviors within stable environments; factories, assembly lines, fast food chains and department stores are good examples. The military is another example of a Mechanistic Organization. Soldiers with the same rank must have the basic skills needed to perform specific tasks required of their method of service. Individual soldiers from different companies, regiments, brigades, or battalions all know how to perform basic tasks and standard operating procedures in exactly the same way. High-ranking officers and non-commissioned officers are expected to do the thinking, while "grunts" are expected to follow orders.

## Human Relations School

During the Industrial Revolution, many workers were replaced with machines. This dehumanization of work led to increases in unemployment and poverty. After the stock market crash, the credibility of business was low and feelings of exploitation were high. Eventually, unions and government regulations reacted to the rather dehumanizing effects of Scientific Management Theory and Administrative/Bureaucratic Theory, giving birth to the Human Relations Movement (popular from 1930 through today).

The Hawthorne studies conducted in the 1920s and 1930s by Elton Mayo, at the Hawthorne Works Plant of the Western Electric Company in Chicago, were first designed to explore relationships between working conditions and fatigue, boredom and productivity. There were many types of experiments conducted, but the purpose of the original experiments was to study the effect of lighting on workers' productivity. The study surveyed employees about the lighting conditions in their work space, made lighting changes, and studied productivity. Researchers found that productivity almost always increased after a change in illumination, no matter the type of illumination. They experimented on other changes and again found that no matter the change in conditions, productivity increased. As the research progressed, it began to focus on many other variables such as the attitudes of employees and the social environment outside of work (Morgan, 1997). They ended the experiments when they realized something they couldn't account for—the presence of the researchers—was affecting productivity. This is now known as the Hawthorne Effect.

The studies themselves have been a source of criticism, but they created an evolutionary step, an important milestone in industrial and organizational psychology and in organizational behavior. These studies contributed the idea that workers' productivity was affected by how they were treated and listened to, and how they felt about their work and their coworkers (Osland, et al, 2001). They caused paradigm-shattering breakthroughs in understanding the fact that asking employees about their work environment, paying attention to them, and listening to their feedback could positively affect productivity. This new idea, and the change in understanding it inspired, propelled the development of the Human Relations School.

The Human Relations School was an argument or backlash against viewing workers as automatons, a good example of a self-generating oppositional system where one side of a system produced the existence of the other (Morgan, 1997). Under this theory, more attention was given to individuals and their unique capabilities in the organization. A major belief was that the organization would prosper if its workers prospered as well. Human Resource departments were added to organizations.

The behavioral sciences played a strong role in helping to understand the needs of workers and how the needs of an organization and its workers could be better aligned. Various new theories were spawned, many based on the behavioral sciences.

The Human Relations School stresses the importance of understanding human motivation in the workplace. It assumes that employee motivation is a result of recognition, encouragement, and rewarding of individual contributions. According to Human Relations Theory, ideal managers are those who pay attention to people's social needs and elicit their ideas about work issues.

## Contingency Approach Theory

Contingency Approach Theory has established itself as a dominant perspective in modern organizational analysis. It is situational leadership. We call it the "it depends" approach. It holds that organizations, like organisms, must adapt and evolve in response to a changing environment. Individuals, groups, cultures, industries, technologies, personalities, managerial styles, environments, past experiences, and situations can all vary enormously, so choosing the best managerial approach to take in a given situation varies according to the unique situation (Osland, et al, 2001).

Ideal contingency managers can identify and manipulate a mixture of variables, which may be successful for particular situations. Variables that are thought to be related to success include managerial principles, environment, attitudes, human relationships, and job duties. The Contingency Approach Theory believes that there is no single "best way" of managing. The appropriate strategy depends on the type of task or environment with which one is dealing. The point of Contingency Approach Theory is that different approaches to management may be necessary to perform different tasks within the same organization (Morgan, 1997).

## Organic Organizations

In contrast to Mechanistic Organizations, Organic Organizations are flexible, decentralized systems with broadly defined tasks. Individuals within Organic Organizations communicate directly with anyone in the company instead of following a clear and vertical chain of communication. In Organic Organizations, all employees contribute to the common mission of the organization. Tasks are broadly defined. Knowledge, information, power, and control are decentralized. Teams may be cross-functional and cross-hierarchical. In Organic Organizations, there is a low level of formalization and a high level of horizontal communication (Osland, et al, 2001). Organic organizational structure is best suited for complex, dynamic environments that require flexibility and creativity. Ideal managers of organizations are empowering and have flexible styles.

## Open Systems Theory

Open Systems Theory became popular due to the rapidly changing environment of the mid-1960s, when effective managers understood the interdependence among the different individuals and subsystems of an organization and recognized that organizations themselves are a part of greater systems in the environment. Open Systems Theory, which takes its main inspiration from the work of Ludwig von Bertalanffy, a theoretical biologist, is grounded in the metaphor of Organic Organizations. Organizations, like organisms, depend on a wider environment for various kinds of sustenance. They are "open" to the environment and must achieve an appropriate relationship with that environment if they are to survive (Morgan, 1997).

Open Systems Theory emphasizes the environment in which organizations exist, the relationships between interrelated subsystems, and the practical use of subsystems to identify and eliminate potential dysfunctions (Morgan, 1997). Ideal managers are the interface between these subsystems. The ideal manager is a systems thinker, having the ability to understand the interdependent relationships between subsystems. The ideal manager can see and predict how a change in one system can cause changes in other systems (Osland, et al, 2001).

## Total Quality Management

*Learning is not compulsory…neither is survival.*
*—W. Edwards Deming*

Total Quality Management (TQM) is a management strategy aimed at embedding awareness of quality in all organizational processes. It has been widely applied in business, government, and education. It is a people-focused management system centered on continual improvement and customer satisfaction.

26

W. Edwards Deming based TQM on five principles:

1. Power is shared by all involved.
2. The "hands-on" workers share ideas for improvement with leaders, and leaders share their ideas with workers.
3. Responsibilities are shared among all people in the organization.
4. Attention to customer satisfaction is paramount, and quality is achieved by focusing on doing even the small things right the first time.
5. Finally, improvement is constant, even when the organization is experiencing success.

TQM was and still is very influential. It caused paradigm-shifting breakthroughs, and was very influential on modern leadership philosophy. The progressive ideas of W. Edwards Deming's TQM Theory created a groundbreaking school of thought that paved the way for Peter Senge's articulation of the Learning Organization (the topic of chapter 4).

### Try This: Personal Leadership Theory Statement

Create your own personal leadership theory statement. How do you feel about people in general? Go back through the theories in this chapter picking bits and pieces that you agree with and think are relevant. Take the main theoretical ideas you agree with and weave them together with your own thoughts and ideas. Finally, tell the story. Describe what your program or organization would look like if it operated under the personal leadership theory you articulated. As you explore the topics in this book you can expand and refine your statement.

### Foundation of Values

*Leadership is a potent combination of strategy and character. But if you must be without one, be without the strategy.*
—*General H. Norman Schwarzkopf*

*Men of genius are admired, men of wealth are envied, men of power are feared; but only men of character are trusted.*
—*Alfred Adler*

We have described many leadership ideas that can be used as part of your theoretical leadership foundation. We encourage you to build your personal philosophy of leadership on foundations of strong leadership theory, but that is not enough. The solid foundation of a truly great organization is not theory, but its mission, values, and ethics. In our organization we say, "Our values are the boss." We use our values to guide our policy development and decision making. We do not make decisions based on fear or greed, but on our values.

## How to Be: Ethical Ideals

*Nearly all men can stand adversity, but if you want to test a man's character, give him power.*
*—Abraham Lincoln*

Ethical leaders constantly study the emerging base of knowledge about leadership and demonstrate this knowledge in their professional leadership and development. They make decisions based on what is in the best interest of key stakeholders. They provide insight and information for the continual evaluation and improvement of programs or services through the appropriate channels in a committed effort to provide a high standard of service in all endeavors. They promote the individual successes of their followers through the guidance and mentoring of a supervisor or peer, and applicable training opportunities. They work toward retaining a stable workforce through equitable compensation (salary, benefits, working conditions, and schedules) for their employees.

Ethical leaders in the child care and youth development profession are critically reflective practitioners, continually learning and revising their practices based on the growing field of knowledge in child development. They aim to best provide for the safety and improvement of services to children and families, and meet the changing needs of the organization or program, as well as the key stakeholders of the profession. They make program and leadership decisions based on the best interest of the children and their organizations.

They provide the community with high-quality services, ensuring that every child has access to programs that are developmentally appropriate. Leaders create programs that enable children and youth to participate fully in carefully planned environments that are safe and healthy and facilitate individual progress in social, emotional, physical and cognitive development. Leaders recognize and accept the uniqueness of each child by respecting race, ethnicity, gender, ability, religion, and socio-economic status. Ethical leaders are honest and fair in their interactions with each child. Leaders plan environments that are free from physical or mental harm. They promote a sense of well-being for each child through a clearly articulated structure with guidelines and procedures.

They collaborate and maintain cooperation among agencies that share responsibility for the general welfare of children and families. They strive toward greater social acknowledgment of children's rights, including their rights to adequate food, shelter, health care, education, and nurturing environments.

Ethical leaders develop relationships of mutual trust with the families they serve, and respect the dignity of each family, recognizing their uniqueness of culture, ethnicity, language, customs, and beliefs. They recognize different value systems and respect the rights of families to make decisions for their children. They share information with families that demonstrates the child's participation in the child care and youth development program.

Ethical leaders provide nurturing environments through policies and conditions that promote the development of mutual respect and trust, safeguard individual differences, foster positive self and professional development, and celebrate the goals and achievements of coworkers. They respond ethically in all situations by developing and maintaining the principles of honesty, integrity, trust, and respect of individual diversity in relationships with others. They work collaboratively and cooperatively with others in an atmosphere of trust that encourages the dialog and information exchange that promotes the accomplishment of their mission and the realization of their vision.

## How to Act: Walking the Talk

*No change of circumstances can repair a defect of character.*
—*Ralph Waldo Emerson*

Ethical leaders only offer to provide services for which they have the competence, qualifications, and resources. They collaborate and cooperate with schools, health and social service agencies, community groups, and other professionals that work with key stakeholders.

They are familiar with the laws and regulations that pertain to their field of service. They learn how the government processes work in order to advocate for their stakeholders. They recognize, support, follow, and advocate for policies and laws that promote the well-being of their stakeholders. In cases of violation, upon becoming aware of the situation, they take the necessary and appropriate action as stipulated by law. They report suspicion of child abuse or neglect as outlined by law. They report unethical practices of any organization to the person responsible for that program.

They provide a workplace that is safe and emotionally supportive. In a spirit of professional pride and fellowship, they recognize and celebrate the growth and development of their colleagues through support and encouragement of their goals and achievements. They acknowledge and utilize the experience and education of staff, and they encourage their staff's continued development by providing opportunities for training, mentoring, and professional and personal growth.

Ethical leaders address issues of behavioral concerns or disagreements with coworkers in a way that is dignified, honest and respectful. They make statements that specifically address issues of firsthand knowledge that are relevant to key stakeholders. In every situation, they speak and act in a manner that is reflective of the core values of honesty, trust, and respect.

Tragically, in many programs, people are hired to be "warm bodies." Their job is to keep the kids safe—no more. Ethical leaders only hire individuals that are suited for and professionally trained in working with school-age children. They develop and utilize the experience and education of staff. They encourage continual development of skills by providing opportunities for training in child development, guidance, health and safety, learning environments, working with families, special needs, diversity, curriculum development, etc.

Leaders focus on the strengths and assets of each family unit. They select honestly and fairly that information about a child's participation in the child care and youth development program that needs to be shared with the family. They work with conflicting family members without becoming an advocate for any particular person. They provide activities that honor diversity and build on children's experiences.

They show loyalty and support for the policies and reputation of the program, except in cases that endanger children/youth or violate laws and regulations designed to protect children/youth. They promote the program through positive dialog and behaviors. They refrain from making inappropriate comments or acting in a non-professional way in the community.

Ethical leaders provide programs that facilitate the healthy development of each child enrolled in their programs. They develop programs that meet the needs of the community and families they serve. They establish and/or participate in organizations that further the development of other child care and youth development professionals. They walk the talk!

## Ethical Dilemma: The Thieving Thespian

Imagine that you work in an organization providing multi-site afterschool programs. You work with a team of eight directors. One of the directors acts like the "perfect professional" any time the big boss is present. But when the boss leaves, the director does as little as humanly possible and complains about everything, especially about how little he gets paid. Yesterday when the supervisor was out of the office, you saw this director going through the boss's desk. You figured he was just looking around, being lazy, so he didn't have to do any real work. When you asked him about it, he said he was looking for a tissue. You figured that was his lamest excuse yet! Today, however, your boss announced that a substantial amount of money had been stolen from the office yesterday. She wanted anyone with information that might help to catch the thief to speak up and help with the investigation. What do you do?

a. Who are the stake-holders in this scenario?
b. Analyze your choices and their impact on ALL the stake-holders.
c. What are the ethical issues at stake in this scenario? What is the most ethical decision?
d. What is the best way to enact this decision and what skills are necessary to complete it effectively?

## Ethical Dilemma: A Rose By Any Other Name...

Your program is in need of additional funds, and you are the one to go to the big boss and ask for them. In your discussion with her she makes the suggestion that your program change its name so that it won't be confused with a "baby-sitting club." In doing so, she thinks it will create more interest in directing funds to your program. Currently, your program is called "School-Age Child Care." She suggests that you change the program's name to "Out of School Education." You believe that the term, "School-Age Child Care" accurately describes the philosophy of your program. Your understanding of "CARE" is that it stands for "Creating Adventures in Recreation and Education." You think that the proposed new name undermines that philosophy. On the other hand, you need more money. What do you do?

a. Who are the stake-holders in this scenario?
b. Analyze your choices and their impact on ALL the stake-holders.
c. What are the ethical issues at stake in this scenario? What is the most ethical decision?
d. What is the best way to enact this decision and what skills are necessary to complete it effectively?

## Try This: Character Activity
### Choosing Character Quotes Ice Breaker
You'll need twenty index cards. Write one half of each of the following quotes on each card. On "GO" the participants move around the room and find the person with the other half of their quote. When partners find each other, they discuss what the quote means to their lives and their work. When finished, go around the room and have partners read their quotes and share some of that they discussed.

1. *Character may be manifested in the great moments, but it is made in the small ones.*
—*Phillips Brooks*

2. *The good man is the man who, no matter how morally unworthy he has been, is moving to become better.*
—*John Dewey*

3. *Character cannot be developed in ease and quiet. Only through experiences of trial and suffering can the soul be strengthened, vision cleared, ambition inspired and success achieved.*
—*Helen Keller*

4. *I look to a day when people will not be judged by the color of their skin, but by the content of their character.*
—*Martin Luther King, Jr.*

5. *No man is fit to command another that cannot command himself.*
—*William Penn*

6. *Leaders get out in front and stay there by raising the standards by which they judge themselves—and by which they are willing to be judged.*
—*Frederick W. Smith*

7. *Character builds slowly, but it can be torn down with incredible swiftness.*
—*Faith Baldwin*

8. *All honor's wounds are self-inflicted.*
—*Andrew Carnegie*

9. *To educate a man in mind and not in morals is to educate a menace to society.*
—*Theodore Roosevelt*

10. *Character is like a tree and reputation its shadow. The shadow is what we think it is; the tree is the real thing.*
—*Abraham Lincoln*

## Try This: Ethical Audit

Conduct an ethical audit of your employment policies. Read them with the perspective of your values and ethics. Are they based on fear or greed, or are they based on genuine caring and respect?

## Try This: Put First Things First

Put your values first in your organization. Put the interests of the children, their families, your employees, and their families first. Put your mission first. Put quality first. When you do this, your business will succeed. Put first things first and trust the systems to build a better business.

## Conclusion

*Character is the firm foundation stone upon which one must build to win respect. Just as no worthy building can be erected on a weak foundation, so no lasting reputation worthy of respect can be built on a weak character.*
*—R. C. Samsel*

*If you have built castles in the air, your work need not be lost; that is where they should be. Now put foundations under them.*
*—Henry David Thoreau*

In real-world construction of a building the foundation must be laid before construction of the rest of the building can begin. You may work in an organization that was built with no leadership foundation or an ineffective foundation. As a leader it is never too late to lay a new foundation or to change an existing foundation. The essence of leadership is continuous learning and revising your theoretical foundation based on new learning.

Share a summary of the theories in this chapter with your work team. Have a discussion about which comes closest to your current style. Create a description of their perception of the ideal leader. Now develop a new foundation and build your leadership style on your new foundation.

When Chelsea was traveling in Europe, she had the chance to view a beautiful tapestry, a metaphor for leadership. The overall picture struck her consciousness first. It was so wonderful that it seemed magical. As she drew nearer to the tapestry itself, it gradually became apparent that the picture had been created by minute, precise formations in the weave, intricate combinations of color, tint, and hue. Miniature shapes, so small they were nearly invisible to the naked eye, merged into larger patterns, which themselves merged into even larger images, in an ever-expanding process until the overall picture was finally created. Close inspection revealed that the fine tapestry was the result of careful, exacting process applied by a master.

This is also true when walking into an organization of an effective leader. At first glance, all that is visible are active people, engaged in an appropriate task, possibly smiling, enjoying themselves while they learn and interact with others. Yet like the tapestry, a closer look can be quite revealing. The creation of a great organization is not the result of simple happenstance, rather it is the effect of the careful integration of vision, goals, images, words, ideas, and culture by a creative, empowering leader dedicated to developing people.

In time, your own personal leadership philosophy will be itself a tapestry that weaves together the appropriate components, creating an apparently seamless picture of vision, effective, practices, learning, feedback, coaching, and caring values that are all but invisible to the untrained eye. Like the art of weaving a tapestry, effective leadership is indeed a learnable skill, a combination of bits and pieces that can be mastered by anyone interested and willing to learn, given the necessary guidance and skills.

This poem fits with our metaphor of leadership being a built on a foundation of values and well-laid plans. It is consistent with the role a genuine and ethical leader plays—to be constructive, and build people up, not tear them down.

*I watched them tearing a building down,*
*    a gang of men in a busy town.*
*With a "Ho, Heave, Ho" and a lusty yell,*
*    they swung the beam and a side wall fell.*
*I asked the foreman, "Are those men skilled*
*    as the one's you'd hire if you had to build?"*
*He laughed and said, "No indeed,*
*    a common laborer is all I need*
*And I can wreck in a day or two*
*    what the builders have taken a year to do."*
*I thought to myself as I went my way,*
*    "Which of these roles have I to play?*
*Am I patiently doing the best that I can,*
*    measuring my life by a well laid plan,*
*Am I a builder who works with skill and care,*
*    building others up by the rule and square*
*Or am I a wrecker as I walk the town*
*    content with the task of tearing down."*

## Discussion Questions

1. What theory or theories best describes the philosophy of your current organization?

2. Have you worked for organizations or leaders whose philosophies seem to be based in some of these theories? As the worker, how did you feel?

3. Think about the pros and cons of each theory. What kind of combination of theories could you blend together to eliminate the cons and enhance the pros? What new problems might you create with this new philosophy?

4. How do ethical behaviors (poor or good) influence child care programs and the child care profession?

5. To what degree do you think your organization or program(s) discusses ethical issues that confront your profession?
6. What are some ethical issues or dilemmas that you have faced as a leader?

7. To what degree do you think your constituents feel your organization or program is one of integrity and high ethical quality? What do you think influences that perception?

## Helpful Resources

Some of the Story Times and discussion questions, and all of the ethical ideals and practices presented in this chapter, are adapted from the Code of Ethics for School-Age Care (Charron, 2001). The School-Age Care Department of Concordia University no longer exists. The Code of Ethics was created by students and professors in that department: Rosa Andrews, Ellen Clippinger, Nancy Dougherty, Carmen Gatti, Anne Gleason, Lisa Shaffer, and Lori J.N. Charron, PhD. Download the entire code of ethics which includes many case studies, ethical dilemmas, and discussion questions at www.ctafterschoolnetwork.org/documents/Code_of_Ethics_for_SAC.pdf

Download the National Afterschool Association Code of Ethics at http://naaweb.yourmembership.com/resource/resmgr/naacodeofethicsjan09.pdf

Create and live by your personal mission statement. Link to the Franklin Covey Mission Builder exercise at www.franklincovey.com/msb/

## Reference Notes

Charron, L. (Ed.). (2001). *Code of ethics for school-age care.* (SAC Monograph No. 1). St. Paul, MN: Concordia University, Concordia School of Human Services.

Darling-Hammond, L. (1997). *The right to learn: A blue print for creating schools that work.* San Francisco, CA: Jossey-Bass Publishers.

Hearron, P., & Hildebrand, V. (2007). *Management of child development centers, 6th edition.* Upper Saddle River, NJ: Pearson Education, Inc.

Kaufman, D. L. (1980). Systems: *An introduction to systems thinking.* Minneapolis, MN: S.A. Carlton

Kim, D. H. (1994). *Systems archetypes I.* Cambridge, MA: Pegasus Communications.

Koffman F., & Senge, P. (1995). Communities of commitment: The heart of learning organizations. In S. Chawla & J. Renesch (Eds.), *Learning Organizations* (p. 15–43). Portland, OR: Productivity Press.

Lawler, E. (1992). *The ultimate advantage: Creating the high-involvement organization.* San Francisco: Jossey-Bass Publishers.
Morgan, G. (1997). *Images of organization.* Thousand Oaks, CA: Sage Publications, Inc.

Osland, J., Kolb, D., & Rubin, I. (2001). *Organizational behavior: An experiential approach.* Upper Saddle River, NJ: Prentice Hall.
Senge, P. M. (1990). *The fifth discipline: The art and practice of the learning organization.* New York, NY: Doubleday.

Vaill, P. (1996). *Learning as a way of being: Strategies for survival in a world of permanent white water.* San Francisco, CA: Jossey-Bass Publishers.

# Chapter 3: Playing the Part

*The art of communication is the language of leadership.*
—James Humes

*We're following the leader wherever he may go.*
—The Lost Boys, Peter Pan

## Introduction

*The most dangerous leadership myth is that leaders are born—that there is a genetic factor to leadership. This myth asserts that people simply either have certain charismatic qualities or not. That's nonsense; in fact, the opposite is true. Leaders are made rather than born.*
—Warren G. Bennis

We can be visionary by looking toward the future, and we learn a lot by studying the past, but the present gives us the opportunity to apply what we have learned. We have to be leaders, make decisions, and influence people in the here and now. The opportunity to shape the future exists in the present. The present is the stage on which we must play the part of the leader.

You do not have to be an expert in leadership to practice leadership or to take on a leadership endeavor. You do not have to know all the answers—quite the contrary. In fact, no matter how many books you read on leadership, how many classes on leadership you attend, or how many leaders you talk with, you will not be perfect. You will make mistakes.

Reading about leadership can never take the place of experiencing it. Sometimes people have to experience something before they believe it. Tell someone there are 500 billion stars in the sky and he'll believe you. Tell him a wall has wet paint, and he has to touch it for himself!

Leadership must be learned from the stage, not from the audience, and mistakes are a valuable part of learning. In order to become a great leader, you must begin to play the part. Do not expect to win any Academy Awards in your first performance.

You must spend time learning the part, developing the character, practicing it in high school drama and in community theatre before you are ready for Broadway or Hollywood. Use every experience and every mistake to perfect your craft.

Time and energy spent improving your leadership performance are wise investments. As you grow and learn, you will feel confident to audition for bigger leadership roles, maybe even title roles. As you develop you will be offered more and higher-paying leadership roles. A talent scout for the leadership world might even discover you, and make you rich and famous. What is in this for you? More success, more power, more control, more growth, more learning, more influence, and more money! Learning to develop your leadership skills will help you in virtually every aspect of your life.

We begin this chapter with a discussion of leadership in general. We believe that three of the most basic and most critical skills for a leader to develop are communication skills, management skills, and coaching skills. After exploring each of these basic skill sets we will bring the discussion home to the field of child care and youth development.

We begin with the fundamental point that leadership is not something done by the ONE person designated as the leader in a program or organization. Leadership is a function shared by ALL members of an organization. Leadership can be learned, but not everyone is interested in or capable of becoming a great leader.

In an effective intentional organization, every person functions as both a leader and a follower at different times. Leadership is the process of influencing others to understand and agree about what needs to be done and how it can be done effectively. It is the process of making it easier for individuals and teams to accomplish the shared mission and goals (Yukl, 2002). Every member of a child care or youth development organization shares in this function. The agency director, the site directors, the caregivers, and the children all function as leaders at times.

A widely-held myth of leadership is that the "people who get to the top are leaders." People who achieve top levels of management sometimes do so because of authentic leadership, but sometimes they do so because of popularity with other top-level officials, preferential treatment, politics, or pure nepotism. Leadership and superior position are not synonymous. Leadership is not a position; it is an action and a process. It involves qualities and skills that are useful whether one is in the executive suite or on the front line, on Wall Street or Main Street (Kouzes & Posner, 1995).

The most basic definition of a leader is someone who has followers. People who get to the top have subordinates, but not necessarily followers. People who get to the top can brandish power and control over their subordinates, but not necessarily exhibit influence. On the other hand, people at all levels of an organization can have followers over whom they can effectively and positively exhibit influence. Every member of our organization at every level of the organization is expected to be a leader.

Effective leaders of the future need the willingness and ability to involve others, share power and control, inspire high levels of motivation and emotional strength, and model extraordinary levels of perception and insight into the world and into themselves (Schein, 1996). In the quickly changing business environment, the intellectual functions of a leader are increasingly important. Effective leaders need significant brainpower and the mental agility to think through problems and generate effective solutions.

## Story Time: The Role We Play
*Leadership is the ability to hide your panic from others.*

After new program directors have been employed for a couple of weeks, Chelsea always tells them the same story about how she learned to play the role of leader. This is her story. I was a new assistant director at an early childhood center. I was also new to the field so I knew very few people and very little about the "big issues." I attended a gathering of early childhood "big wigs" with my director. I was very intimidated and told her I didn't think I ought to be there.

She said, "Chelsea, these people don't know you. Listen to their conversations, nod your head occasionally, and ask questions. Pick up a couple of tidbits of facts. As you mingle, use these tidbits to add to the next conversation. No one will know that you feel like an imposter on the inside. Fake it 'til you make it." So I took her advice and played the part.

She was right. No one seemed to catch on as long as I avoided being asked in-depth questions. A few years later, I attended a similar gathering. This time I knew quite a few people. I joined in on many conversations. At one point, I heard myself talking about an important early childhood issue as if I knew what I was saying, and thought, "That sounded pretty good. Was that me?" It was at that point that I realized I DID know what I was talking about. I wasn't faking it anymore.

Usually, when I get through telling this story, the new program director will nod his or her head, accepting the information, but not too sure what to do with it. After about a year or so on the job, most directors come back to us to report that they now know exactly what that story was, and they excitedly report that they no longer feel like they are faking it. Success at "faking it until you make it" hinges on what we perceive our role and purpose to be. This story makes a point about how we define our purpose—the role we play.

We all have parts to play, hats to wear, both in our personal and professional lives. As leaders in child care and youth development organizations, it is essential for us to keep the big picture in our perspective. We must remember the vital role we play in our programs and in our organizations and remember our values, mission, and vision. We choose this profession so we can make a difference, and be part of building healthier children, healthier families, and healthier communities.

## The Role "Leader"

Chelsea's advice was, "Fake it 'til you make it"? Fake it? Fake what? In order to play the part well, you need more character development and research. You must really explore this part. Pretend you have been hired to play a role in a play or television show. You have been offered the part of "The Leader." To play the role, you need to know the "motivation" and description of the character. Here it is.

The Leader (male or female): You are very creative, and have a unique style and a unique perspective. You express yourself well. You appreciate aesthetics and the beauty in things around you. Your creativity gives you limitless thinking skills and open-mindedness. You are imaginative and eager to try new things, test theories, and take risks. You enjoy creating and displaying your work. You are bold and confident. You are thoughtful and reflective and innovative; a dreamer. You imagine the impossible, see things in a different light, and think outside the box.

You have the ability to translate vision into reality and transfer your vision to others. You believe in other people, attract and keep followers, and create new leaders. You inspire and motivate rather than intimidate. You encourage and empower others. You believe in people and in yourself.

You have a strong moral character, integrity, and high personal standards. You have a strong internal focus of control, maturity, and personal integrity. You are self-disciplined and trustworthy. You never sit yourself above others, except in taking responsibility. You lead by example. You walk the talk, and deliver more than you promise.

You set high standards and expectations, yet you have the ability to "step on someone's toes without messing up their shine." You communicate well, listen well, and make great decisions. You are assertive, dependable, decisive, cooperative, energetic, persistent, and alert to the social environment.

You have a high energy level, self-confidence, high stress tolerance, and strong interpersonal skills. You exude energy, enthusiasm, and determination. You influence others and make an impact on people. You take action while others hesitate.

This is a large, challenging part to play. Please do not feel like giving up after reading this. Think about it in terms of baby steps. The best place to start is with the foundation of trustworthiness. For people to follow, you must gain their trust. That does not mean you never make mistakes. In fact, making mistakes can help people trust you more as long as you handle those mistakes effectively. Being trustworthy means that your staff trusts that you have a plan and know how to get there. They trust you will take care of them along the way. They trust you will get them out of a mess; you have their back. You gain this trust by being consistent, upfront, and real. Hold people accountable for their behavior. Do this with everyone so that each of your followers knows you will call them on their actions and will do the same for any of their coworkers as well as yourself. Once you gain their trust, so many of the other traits we discussed earlier will be much easier to master.

## Communication Skills

*Wise men speak because they have something to say. Fools speak because they have to say something.*
*—Plato*

*Yakety yak, don't talk back!*
*—The Coasters*

Communication is an exchange or sharing of ideas. It is the essence of social interaction. It is the basis of how we see the world and how the world responds to us. We live in a world filled with other people. We live together, work together, and play together. In our personal lives, we need each other for security, comfort, friendship, and love. In our working environment, we need each other in order to achieve our goals and objectives. None of these goals can be achieved without communication.

Communication is the oil of the proverbial "well-oiled machine." It makes all the parts of an operation run smoothly and effectively. Communication is the basic thread that ties us together. Through communication, we make known our needs, our wants, our ideas, and our feelings. The better we are at communicating, the more effective we are at achieving our hopes and dreams.

When we communicate, we extend something of ourselves into others and take back a part of them. Effective communication is good for interpersonal relationships and organizational effectiveness. It makes growth and change possible, but involves two risks: we may expose what we really are inside, and we may possibly change into something different.

Poor communication skills are at the core of many frustrating relationship problems, whether with coworkers, friends, spouses, children, or authority figures. Barriers, which limit our ability to relate to others, can include fear, impatience, inattentiveness, biases, mistaken assumptions, power and role issues, mistrust, personal behaviors, environmental considerations, and level of understanding.

Communication pitfalls happen when we become unconscious about what we say to others or how we say it. If we are thoughtful about these pitfalls and how they are detrimental to our relationships, then we can make a conscious choice about what we say, how we say it, and how we choose to listen.

We could write an entire book about how to effectively communicate. Believe us; we have learned so much just by being married and by working to stay married! But we know that communication is just one aspect of leadership, so we have just picked our most important seventeen strategies and pitfalls to include here.

**Seventeen Important Communication Strategies and Pitfalls**

1. Before you open your mouth, W.A.I.T.—that stands for Why Am I Talking. Be clear in your own mind what you want to communicate to others. Think about it and script it out before you speak or write. This is the natural style of the introvert, but it can be especially important and extremely effective for all people when preparing for conversations we know may be difficult.

2. Be accountable. When we are accountable, we know that we are in charge of our life and how we perceive it. No one else can make us do or feel anything. Accountability adds power to our relationships. If we are accountable, there is no room for blame. When we are accountable, we have room to choose our experience of a situation and then move forward with clarity. Don't say, "She made me feel bad"; instead say "I chose to perceive that as personal." Don't say, "He hurt my feelings"; instead say, "I let my feelings be hurt."

3. What you HEARD is not what I SAID! Strategic planning for the "what" and the "how" of communication can help prevent this. It has been said that when two people talk to each other, six voices are heard:
   - What you THINK you say.
   - What you actually DO say.
   - What the other person THINKS you say.

- What the other person THINKS he says.
- What the other person actually DOES say.
- What you THINK the other person says.

4. Get to know how the other person communicates. Not everyone thinks or communicates the same way. It is important to know gender, cultural, and individual differences in communication styles, as well as individual communication strengths of the listener. Communicate with others, not in the way you want them to communicate with you, but in the way THEY want you to communicate with them.

5. Say what you mean. Be specific! Vagueness and imprecise language are useless. Speaking the facts allows a clear solution to occur as well as the opportunity for action. Specifics let others know exactly what you want and need. Clarity in our language lets us be more affirmative, direct and effective.

6. Don't dilute yourself. Don't bring up an issue that is important and then dilute it by saying, "But it's not a big deal," or "But we all could be better at that." This passive, wimpy style lowers your effectiveness and thereby lowers your self-esteem. It encourages others to take advantage of you.

7. Be objective and presume positive intentions. Don't presume that because someone does something that makes you angry that the person doesn't care about you. When you communicate an issue, explain what you actually observed or heard and then ask the person to explain his/her intentions, and if necessary specify a more acceptable option. Describe problems in terms of the behavior you see and the standards of behavior you expect. Describe the behavior you see, its consequences, and your feelings without making accusations and attributing motives.

8. Express only what YOU feel. Don't say or write, "Shirley is really angry with you." Often when this happens, that person goes back to confront Shirley, who says she wasn't angry, but then Shirley gets angry with the person who said that she was. Communicate what YOU feel and let Shirley communicate what she feels.

9. No sideways communicating. In the most destructive form this is gossip. If you have something you wish to communicate about another person, start by communicating it directly with that person. If you need a "sounding board" to rehearse what and how you will communicate, choose a friend or family member who does not relate with the other person, or choose a supervisor. It is not appropriate to talk to the person's peers or subordinates in a negative way.

10. The situation will not go away if you ignore it or avoid it. There are several approaches to take in a conflict resolution situation: forcing/competing, accommodating, compromising, collaborating, and avoiding. Unless tempers are high, avoidance is not the best choice. Avoidance results in frustration from lack of resolution, and it encourages others to use your chosen technique when they need to communicate with you. In other words, if you avoid others, they will avoid you.

11. Say it or stuff it. Don't punish others because you are avoidant. Don't become passively aggressive; don't gossip; don't sulk or pout; don't seek revenge; don't ignore people. If you can't respectfully and assertively communicate your issue, then suck it up and get over it.

12. Use non-verbal communication. Research indicates that 65 percent of our communication is nonverbal (Burgoon, Buller, & Woodall, 1989). Don't limit yourself to verbal communication. Develop skills in facial expression, tone of voice, and body language. Look interested. Reduce the level of distraction; putting away work or closing a door may send a non-verbal message that you are ready to listen. In written communication, take care to convey the emotion you want. Since written communication is void of emotion, misunderstanding the emotional context is a potential problem.

13. Maintain eye contact. It has been said that males listen with their ears, not their eyes. Males sometimes need to work harder at maintaining eye contact than females, to which it comes more naturally. But eye contact can be interpreted as aggression when the conversation becomes heated. So remember: not when hot! When it gets "hot," breaking eye contact may help to diffuse the anger.

14. Listen well. Silence is one great art of communication. Listen to the true meaning of others. Listen with your whole body. Press your lips together. Sometimes attentive silence is best; giving the speaker uninterrupted time to say what needs to be said. It may be appropriate to ask questions for clarification but be careful to avoid asking questions that detract from the speaker's main point. Ask open-ended questions. If a speaker has come to you at a time when you cannot give her your full attention, consider letting her know that and setting a specific time to converse.

15. Confirm and clarify. Listen reflectively. Paraphrasing the words, meaning, and emotions of the speaker acknowledges that you understand and provides the opportunity to correct any misunderstandings. Probe for increased understanding by saying, "Please say more about…" or "I'm curious about…"

Repeat what you have heard for clarification. Make sure you've got it right!
- "Let me see if I've got this right."
- "So what you're saying is…"
- "Wait, I'm not sure I got that! Tell me again!"

Ask clarifying questions to make sure you understand things before responding. It is especially important to do this when people use a label or speak in generalities.
- "What do you mean by 'hyper' (etc.)?" "Can you give me an example?"
- "What did he do and say?" "What did you have in mind?"
- "What was it you were trying to do?" "What have you tried so far?"

16. Acknowledge and affirm emotions: name it! Acknowledge the feeling behind the concern or demand. Learning to acknowledge the other person's reality can be enormously helpful. Whatever turn the dialog takes, it is important that you handle it with respect. Even when they are upset or angry, tell them that you are glad that they called or came to speak with you. Tell them that you can't do anything about a problem you don't know about. Tell them many others might not come and talk to you, and you are glad they did! There are many ways to acknowledge another person, whether a parent, child, caregiver, or colleague:
- Acknowledge a person's feelings.
- Acknowledge a person's situation or reality.

- Acknowledge a person's positive intention or their lack of negative intention.
- Take responsibility for anything you may have done to contribute to the problem.

17. Value and invest in open communication. Realize how important effective communication is in your life. It's about the relationships. Effective communication is a strong part of being an effective leader, follower, spouse, parent, and citizen. Be a student of communication; learn about your communication styles and weaknesses, learn strategies to improve your communication, and then work to implement what you learn into your day-to-day communication strategies.

Communication is like a sewer...what you get out of it depends on what you put into it.

## Story Time: Name It

One of Mike's experiences illustrates the importance of naming it. This is his story. I was in a hotel in Florida doing a keynote session. After eating breakfast in the lobby I went to the elevator to go up to the fourth floor where my session would be. I pushed the up button. I was lost in thought about my session when the door opened. I started to enter the elevator when I realized that someone was exiting. I made eye contact with the guy as we almost bumped into each other. He didn't speak, but gave me a really weird look. I attributed the strange expression on his face to how I almost bumped into him. As the door began to close I realized the real reason behind his expression.

He had just passed gas, made wind, cut the cheese, tooted. It stunk!

I covered my nostrils with one hand and pushed the "4" button with the other. The elevator went up one floor and stopped. I was about to have company.

A woman entered the elevator and the doors closed. She turned and looked at me and squinted her eyes. It was a very awkward moment to say the least. I'm a shy person, so I considered just remaining silent. Then I considered the chance that she might be a member of my audience, so I decided to name it.

I said, "Have you ever gotten in to an elevator and SOMEONE ELSE passed gas? It wasn't me it was the guy before me!" She said, "Yea, right. Good excuse." We both laughed. I don't know if she believed me or not, but I was glad I named it because she was indeed in my audience. I was also glad that it had partially dissipated by the time the elevator opened again.

Sometimes emotions can be like that fart. Someone is mad, frustrated, anxious, or sad. It is out there, and you both know it. It might stink; they might be mad at you when you did nothing wrong. You can ignore it and pretend it is not there, or you can be empathetic.

You can name it by saying, "I can see that this is upsetting to you." By naming it you show that you care and that you are empathetic. By naming it you can also help the emotion to dissipate.

### Story Time: Commuter Communication Consequences
A few years ago Chelsea and I planned a family vacation at Chelsea's family camp "Ondawa" on Silver Lake in New York's Adirondack Mountains. Our plan was to fly into Burlington, Vermont, rent a car, take the ferry across Lake Champlain, and drive to camp. It was a good plan. We booked our ticket to Burlington with a travel agent.

Our flight from Albuquerque included a layover in St. Louis. We found our new gate for the next leg of the flight into Burlington. The monitor at the gate counter said, "Burlington." The sign over the gate doorway said, "Burlington." We boarded the surprisingly small commuter plane to Burlington. When we were up in the air, Chelsea began to wonder why we were on such a small commuter plane from St. Louis, Missouri, all the way to Vermont.

We were in the front row in the plane and the cockpit was open.

Chelsea asked the pilot, "Sir, where is this flight going?" He replied, "Burlington ma'am." Chelsea said, "okay" and leaned back, still a little disconcerted. The pilot said, "What's wrong? Aren't you supposed to be going to Burlington?"

Chelsea said, "Yes we are, but I'm just surprised that such a small plane is going all the way from Missouri to Vermont." The pilot said, "Ma'am this plane is going to Burlington, Iowa."

We quickly concluded that Burlington, Iowa, was not located in Vermont!

We enjoyed meeting all of the nice people in Burlington, Iowa, as we were being rerouted to La Guardia Airport in New York. Eventually we made it to camp.

This story is an example of many communication pitfalls. Be clear in your own mind what you want to communicate to others.

## Management Skills

*So much of what we call management consists of making it difficult for people to work.*
*—Peter F. Drucker*

Leadership experts often contrast management and leadership as follows.
- Managers are efficient. Leaders are effective.
- Managers are concerned with the bottom line. Leaders are concerned with the horizon.
- Managers push. Leaders pull
- Managers control. Leaders trust, motivate, and inspire.
- Managers focus on maintenance. Leaders focus on movement.
- Managers cope with complexity. Leaders cope with change.
- Managers are militaristic. Leaders are democratic.
- Managers plan and budget. Leaders set a direction.
- Managers are surface thinkers. Leaders are systems thinkers.
- Managers organize systems. Leaders align people.
- Managers focus on compliance. Leaders focus on commitment.
- Managers stress obedience. Leaders stress understanding.
- Managers are copies. Leaders are the original.

The point is true—leadership and management describe different skill sets. Leadership skills are a higher order, more sophisticated, more artful set of skills, but I think management skills are suffering from a big image problem here. The choice of words in these comparisons implies that managers are "less than" leaders. Good management skills are important too! Leadership and management are not mutually exclusive.

Leadership is one of the many things that good managers must do. Without good management, systems can become so disorganized and chaotic that they fail to function effectively and eventually break down. Sound management lends a degree of strength, stability, and consistency to complex systems.

Managers must sometimes function as researchers, liaisons, figureheads, spokespersons, entrepreneurs, disturbance handlers, negotiators, crisis managers, supervisors, planners, organizers, decision makers, coordinators, consultants, administrators, and perhaps most importantly...leaders (Yukl, 2002). Managers must sometimes generate and read reports, attend meetings, document background checks, resolve crises, meet with suppliers, meet with boards, comply with IRS requirements, generate payroll, make deposits, account for expenditures, and push paperwork.

And how much do we get paid for all of this?! Then again, money will not make you happy, and happy will not make you money.

The point is that leaders have many management tasks that must be done well in order for the organization to thrive. If these things do not get done in an accurate and professional manner, businesses may fail and managers will not have the opportunity to lead. If these things are not done in an efficient manner, the manager will not have the time to lead. In order to be a good leader, one must first be a good manager. Effective leadership can align all of the human resources together in a way so that many of the important roles and tasks can be shared and accomplished by all of the members of the organization. So, through good leadership, good managers can be more efficient, can better solve surface problems, can better cope with complexity, and can be concerned not only with the bottom line but also with the horizon.

Bennis and Goldsmith say that "The manager does things right; the leader does the right thing" (1997, p. 10). The best leaders can do things right AND do the right thing. As the best leaders learn how to do the right thing (theory), they revise their policies and procedures (practice) to reflect a better way to do things right. Leadership is but one of the things that a great manager does right.

People can be good managers and terrible leaders; they can be good leaders and terrible managers. Years ago, we both worked for someone who was a good manager, but a poor leader. She was a good manager of things—paperwork, facilities, record keeping, and equipment. Her fiscal management skills were very strong, so her branch of the company did better financially than other branches. She had great time-management skills, so she consistently met her deadlines. But she was a poor leader of people. She criticized her employees openly and publicly; she was rude and lacked tact. She was abrasive.

Her actions showed that she truly cared about the building, but not about the people. She focused on the mistakes people made in the past, bringing them up over and over again, but did not help them to avoid mistakes in the future. She was very controlling. She had to "sign off" on the smallest of decisions. She insisted on obedience and she got it when she was looking over her employees' shoulders, but when she turned her back she had neither their obedience nor their respect.

Later we worked for someone else who was a good leader, but a poor manager. He was funny and charismatic. He hosted social events. He showed interest in employees' personal lives. When someone had a personal problem, he tried to help. If an employee had financial problems he would lend them money from his own pocket. He would help the custodian mop the floor. He had a hard work ethic; he was always the first person in the building and the last one to leave.

He always reminded us of the reason for our work—that we were there for the kids and the families. He built strong relationships, so strong that his employees often "covered" for him, hiding his weaknesses. He frequently missed deadlines; grant applications were not submitted on time, so we lost potential funding sources. He lost track of paperwork and records, so his employees sometimes needed to duplicate their work. In the end his poor management skills destroyed relationships and he forfeited the respect he had earned.

## Coaching Skills

*If anything goes bad, I did it. If anything goes semi-good, we did it. If anything goes really good, then you did it. That's all it takes to win.*
*—Paul "Bear" Bryant*

*If you don't know where you're going, you'll end up somewhere else.*
*—Yogi Berra*

From our perspective, good coaches are not merely trainers and cheerleaders, they are leaders. When I think of good coaches, I think about people who have the ability to excite others, to motivate and pump up their teams. I do not think a good coach merely imparts technical skills, teaching the mechanics of the sport. Good coaches deliver "Win one for the Gipper!" speeches that pump up their athletes into a frenzy of energy, enthusiasm, and drive. They can turn the attitude of an entire team around in one half-time motivational speech.

Good coaches teach not only how to play the game, but how to love the game. Good coaches are not the only leader, but develop leadership skills in their players, quarterbacks, and team captains (distributed leadership). When a team wins, the team does not feel the victory belongs to the coach; they say, "We did it!"

A leader that simply imparts technical skills or teaches mechanics is not a good coach. Without the ability to excite others, a coach cannot be effective. Good coaches empower, develop competence, build teamwork, grow character, build up a sense of ownership, and create winning strategies. They rally the entire team around the mission of fair play and winning. These are the traits that effective leaders must have.

Coaches do not do the job themselves; they develop the skills in others. In baseball, when a pitcher is not performing well the coach does not go to the mound and demand the pitcher's ball and glove so that he can take over. He provides feedback. He coaches. Sometimes he replaces the pitcher, but then he goes back to the dugout. When coaches intervene, they do so with questions not answers. Lou Holtz, famed Notre Dame football coach said, "I never learn anything talking. I only learn things when I ask questions."

54

Everyone in an organization must continuously develop their skills in order to succeed at their jobs and meet the changing needs of their colleagues and constituents. When employees increase and improve their skills, it makes the job of the leader easier and more enjoyable, and helps everyone in the organization. The continual development of skills at all levels of an organization is crucial to creating dynamic organizations that adapt to change, grow, and learn.

Not all people want to continually develop themselves. In youth-serving fields, that is not acceptable. It is not acceptable if our kids do not develop and grow while with us. It is not acceptable if our staff does not develop and grow while with us.

Making mistakes is a part of this learning. Taking responsibility for and learning from our mistakes is an essential part of a great organization. No matter how experienced a person is, no one has learned everything there is to know. If our Child Development and Leadership software is version 4.0, there must always be a 4.1 version in development. Olympic athletes, who may be the best in the world in their event, all have coaches who help them. These coaches may not be able to do what the athletes can do, but they know how to observe and help them improve.

## Try This: Coaching Sessions
*Treat a person as he is, and he will remain as he is. Treat him as he could be, and he will become what he should be.*
*—Jimmy Johnson*

Try introducing this to your leadership team and consider making coaching sessions a part of the everyday culture of your organization.

A coaching session is a special five- to seven-minute conversation; an interaction which occurs on a regular basis when the program director works with a site director, when a site director or assistant director works with a caregiver, when a mentor caregiver works with a new caregiver, or even when a caregiver works with a child. The following is a structure and sample language for conducting a coaching session. We have been doing coaching sessions for many years, but we improved our method after attending a workshop with educator and speaker Michael Brandwein (See Helpful Resources and Reference Notes).

Here's what our coaching sessions look like. First we give people what we call "OPPORTUNITIES." These are areas for improvement—new strategies to help them expand their skill level and be more effective at their job. We might say, "I noticed that when you were walking with your group, you were in the middle and some of your kids began to run ahead, while some lagged behind. The further spread out they became, the more stressed you appeared. This is something I learned that worked for me. When I'm transitioning the kids I take the lead and I let the kids know that they don't have to walk in single-file lines—that we can stroll together—but the only rule is they can't get ahead of me. Then, if the group becomes too spread out, I just stop until the group becomes tight again. If you tried that, how do you think it would work?"

Then we share some "GEMS." These are wonderful and effective things we have noticed the person doing that we want to acknowledge specifically and encourage them to keep doing. We provide specific examples, and explain why what they are doing is so valuable, why they should keep doing it, and why it will help accomplish our Mission. We might say something like, "One of the best things I've noticed you doing is that…your relationships with the kids are strong. You get down on their eye level when you talk to them; you use their first names; you really listen to what they say; you show appreciation of their efforts; and you show that you are aware of their special interests." We might ask, "Where did you learn to do this? How do they react when you do this?" We explain why this is important. "When you interact with them like this it really builds a lot of respect and trust. That is going to come back from them to you and it is going to make leading and teaching them so much easier for you, so they are going to learn skills that will serve them well in their lives."

Then we ask if there's anything else they want to talk about or anything else we can do to support them. Finally, we make a plan for action and get a commitment for further development. Both the coach and the learner sign the coaching plan—which quickly becomes routine and no big deal.

Follow-up is important. In a few days the coach might say, "I noticed you moving a group of kids today and they were all really close together and you seemed more relaxed. Tell me about it." Or, "We talked yesterday about being in the lead when transitioning a group of kids. I noticed that again today you were in the middle and again had stragglers and runners. Your group was not being supervised up to our standards. This is now putting your job in jeopardy."

## Bringing It Home

Let's bring this discussion of basic leadership skills back home to the field of child care and youth development. The profession needs more leaders and more effective leaders. Teaching communication skills to children and youth is a strong part of our purpose. Our leaders must have strong written and verbal communication skills and be able to help others in the organization improve their skills. It is difficult for educators to teach skills that they do not possess, and children will learn much more when their role models communicate effectively.

We need good leaders with strong management skills in this profession. Good leadership does not turn its back on the daily roles and tasks of the manager in favor of focusing on ideals and motivating and inspiring people. Good leaders understand the importance of the daily tasks to the big picture. They pay attention to detail. In our profession, leaders must ensure records and documentation are kept for staff and child development. They must ensure facilities are safe and secure. They must ensure staff and events are scheduled properly.

Leadership is all about the followers—the followers who at their best are also leaders. Through coaching followers to thoroughly align themselves with common goals, leaders create a culture that values the necessity of roles and puts tasks in a big-picture perspective, thus moving beyond the need to control and supervise daily roles and tasks. Child care directors can use coaching to continuously develop the skills of everyone in the program.

When the team has been developed to a point where everyone is capable of accomplishing the daily responsibilities typically reserved for the director, more of the daily management roles and tasks are accomplished automatically by the team. Without the need for "pushing" tasks and paperwork, the leader is free to spend time and energy communicating, inspiring, motivating, and "pulling" the team in the direction of accomplishing a mission.

For example, in a child care program, if the director is solely responsible for communicating with parents, or ensuring safety guidelines are followed, then there is a risk of these important tasks being missed in the director's absence. Effective leaders should be able to be away from the center or program without things falling apart. Directors, who must be present to handle all problems, have either robbed their followers of decision-making knowledge, or decision-making authority, or both.

## Try This: Director for a Day

Designate a "director for a day." Give an emerging leader in the program all of your "typical" responsibilities for the day. Let this person know you will be observing him and will give him feedback at the end of the day. Stay on the sidelines and watch. Do not interfere unless there is a big safety or customer service issue. You will not only help develop new leaders with this technique, but you will be able to identify where your followers need more knowledge and information. When you provide the promised feedback to your staff member, together you can identify areas where that person could have done a better job, or made a better decision if he had known more about a situation or had understood a policy or procedure in more detail.

Getting your team to a point where you can "manage by walking around" is in your best interest. This means getting away from the paperwork and the phone and going into the program and informally observing. Do you know what is happening everywhere in the program environment? Sometimes directors rarely leave the entry area of the building. "Floor time" is important for a leader—you need to be out there where the real work is happening. Make sure you know every child's name, every staff member's name, the environments they work in, and their routines.

## Try This: Pick Up a Mop

Some people in leadership positions rarely walk out on the floor—the front lines—where the people of the organization do the work, and when they do, they act as if they are royalty. They expect people to recognize them and give them attention. In a school-age child care program the floor means the program space, where the kids and the caregivers live and learn together. If you are in the type of leadership role where you spend most of your time away from the program, try to modify your schedule so you can get to the program more often. When you do get to the program, look for opportunities to help. Look for equipment that needs to be replaced. Look and listen to the sounds and the relationships. If you are there at clean up time, or when a parent event is ending, help—pick up a mop, take out the trash.

## Conclusion

*Big jobs usually go to the men who prove their ability to outgrow small ones.*
*—Ralph Waldo Emerson*

So what does all this mean? What is the best leadership theory? What is the "best" style of leadership? The best style cannot be defined as one narrowly categorized approach. It is complex and conditional and interrelated—like the tapestry.

If I were forced to describe the best leadership style, I'd say the best method is a holistic and situational style that applies the best practices of many styles in a way that is most effective with unique people existing in a unique state under a unique situation. The best style is flexible and responsible to these unique situations, while being grounded in the consistency of ethical and caring principles. The best style is creative, innovative and exists on a foundation of character, values, and integrity.

The best style is not confined to "in the box" thinking, but is versatile enough to be applied to a variety of situations. It embraces change and is flexible depending on what will be the most effective. The best style is critically reflective, changing in day-to-day practices based on new information, theory and changing situations.

**Discussion Questions**

1. Think about a time in your past when someone successfully and positively coached or guided you or helped you get much better at something that was important to you. This should be a time when you got to a higher level of performance and were comfortable and happy about the experience.

2. What was the skill or thing you learned to do better?

3. Who was the person who helped you?

4. Why was this experience successful for you? What was it about the way the person spoke or acted that made them good at guiding or coaching you? Please come up with as many specific examples of this as you can.

## Helpful Resources

We learned about coaching sessions in an American Camp Association conference workshop with Michael Brandwein. He is an international speaker and trainer whose message is consistent with high-quality child care, school-age care, and camping. Check him out at

www.michaelbrandwein.com

For more information on the American Camp Association conference and resources visit

www.acacamps.org

Peter Drucker is widely known as the father of modern management.
www.druckerinstitute.com

## Reference Notes

Bardwick, Brian Dumaine in "Why Do We Work?" *Fortune*, December 26, 1994, p. 196.

Bennis, W. & Goldsmith, J. (1997). *Learning to lead: A workbook on becoming a leader.* Cambridge, MA: Perseus Books.

Bryson, J. (1995). *Strategic planning for public and nonprofit organization: A guide to strengthening and sustaining organizational achievement.* San Francisco: Jossey-Bass, Inc.

Bryson, J., & Alston, F. (1996). *Creating and implementing your strategic plan: A workbook for public and nonprofit organizations.* San Francisco: Jossey-Bass, Inc. Burgoon, J., Buller, D. & Woodall, W. (1989). *Nonverbal communication: The unspoken dialogue.* New York: Harper and Row.

Charron, L. (Ed.). (2001). *Code of ethics for school-age care.* (SAC Monograph No. 1). St. Paul, MN: Concordia University, Concordia School of Human Services.

Hesselbein, F., Goldsmith, M., & Beckhard, R. (Eds.). *The leader of the future.* San Francisco: Jossey-Bass Publishers.

Kotter, J. (1996). *Leading Change.* Boston: Harvard Business School Press.

McNatt, D. B. (2000). Ancient Pygmalion joins contemporary management: A meta-analysis of the result. *Journal of Applied Psychology*, 85, 314–322.

Smith, Bucklin & Associates, Inc. (2000). *The complete guide to nonprofit management.* New York: John Wiley and Sons, Inc.

Wolf, T. (1999). *Managing a nonprofit organization in the twenty-first century.* New York: Simon and Schuster.

Stogdill, R. M. (1974). *Handbook of leadership: A survey of the literature. New York:* Free Press.

Yukl, G. (2002). *Leadership in organizations.* Upper Saddle River, NJ: Prentice Hall.

# Part III: The Meat

# Chapter 4: Practicing the Art

*A learning organization is a place where people are continually discovering how they create their reality. And how they can change it.*
—Peter Senge

*Education is the mother of leadership.*
—Wendell L. Willkie

*We don't need no education.*
—Pink Floyd

## Introduction

In chapter 2, we discussed many leadership theories: Scientific Management Theory, Administrative Theory, Human Relations School, Contingency Approach, Organic Organizations, Open Systems Theory, and Total Quality Management. Each had their own strengths and weaknesses. Here we take things a step further. Here we will describe an effective and powerful leadership theory—the Learning Organization.

Do you want an innovative, enthusiastic, committed team of people? If so then pay attention to this chapter. Building and implementing the theories of a Learning Organization in your own field of leadership will help you construct that type of team. Learning Organizations promote a sense of ownership and empowerment. Learning Organizations result in better customer service, better decision making, and more creative and innovative thinking strategies. Learning Organizations are dynamic places that are in a constant state of improvement. People in Learning Organizations are responsible and accountable. They interact positively, think on the job, take risks, work cooperatively, seek personal mastery, align themselves with the mission, think systemically, and function as vital participants of the organization. If that sounds good to you keep reading!

*You learn far more from negative leadership than from positive leadership. Because you learn how not to do it. And, therefore, you learn how to do it.*
*—General H. Norman Schwarzkopf*

Let us begin by telling you about our experience working in an organization where the leadership philosophy was NOT like the philosophy we encourage in this book. It was the opposite, the antithesis of a Learning Organization. Chelsea and I both began our professional careers working in a local branch of a large national organization that provided, among other things, school-age child care.

It was a classic hierarchical organization. Authority and control were centralized within a clear, vertical chain of communication and command, and hoarded by the upper-level administrators. "Entry-level employees"—the people who worked directly with the children, the ones who accomplished or didn't accomplish the mission, the people who had direct contact with the people paying for services—were expected to follow policies, procedures, and instructions. They were expected to keep busy and not expected to think. The administrators were expected to do all of the thinking and organizing (the "brains"), and the caregivers were expected to implement their instructions (the "hands").

Only the administrators were trained and educated in child care practices. Knowledge, information about the goals, strategies, budget, and inner workings of the organization were only provided on a "need to know" basis, upper administrators only. Top-level administrators alone had the power to make changes and decisions. They used this power to control lower-level managers and entry-level staff members. Caregivers were treated as mindless automatons.

When problems happened, the leadership of the organization looked at individual parts of the problems ("snapshots"), and failed to see how the solutions they chose would cause additional problems over time, and that the wrong "cures" were often worse than the original disease.

The overwhelming focus was on maximizing profit, yet the strategies implemented to meet this goal often created the opposite effects. If there was not enough profit on the bottom line, reactive and adaptive strategies were developed, which produced big, negative results.

Prices clients paid for services were increased. People were laid off or their work hours were decreased. Staff raises were eliminated. The standard of quality of supplies and equipment was lowered to save money. Budgets for field trips, staff training, snacks, supplies, and equipment were reduced.

As a result of these strategies, quality standards atrophied, staff morale declined, and people left. Turnover was high and whenever a good caregiver quit, the kids who were the most attached to her disenrolled. Without good caregivers, quality decreased, so dissatisfied parents pulled their children out of the program. These events led to decreased income, which led to even worse quality, which was the opposite effect the administration expected from the solutions they implemented.

When we left that organization we hadn't yet heard of the terms "Learning Organization" or "Systems Thinking." We observed the systems in place only partially understanding the power of the destructive systems that were in play. In this chapter we will describe some of the more common systems archetypes in play by using analogies and stories from our experiences and from ecosystems. We'll be talking about manure and mosquitoes; ponies and popcorn; bunnies and bugs; stakeholders and site directors; nature and nurses. Then we'll bring it home to afterschool and early childhood education, to the powerful systems that can enhance and support strong, fiscally stable, top-quality programs. We will discuss how to design a Learning Organization that supports these systems.

The management philosophy of a Learning Organization is based on developing the people—the people who accomplish the mission—in ever-changing organizations. When every individual learns, the organization learns. Organizations that learn benefit from their experience rather than being tossed around in the randomness of a rapidly changing environment (Ollhoff & Walcheski, 2002).

Learning Organizations are grounded by continuous learning and must be led by people who model continuous learning in their own day-to-day behavior. In a Learning Organization, all employees are empowered to learn and to teach.

The Learning Organization is created to learn and grow and change, as opposed to traditional bureaucratic models designed to be stable and predictable in their operations. Learning Organizations are places that individuals "would truly like to work within and which can thrive in a world of increasing interdependency and change" (Kofman & Senge, 1993, p. 32).

Learning Organizations are grounded in three foundations:
- First is a values-based culture. The traditions and customs are based on inspirational human values of love, genuine caring, wonder, humility, respect, and compassion.
- Second, Learning Organizations are places where generative conversations take place. Conversations are not dominated by what has been done in the past and what has or has not worked long ago; rather, people talk about what can be done differently and what can be done better in the future to accomplish the mission and realize the vision. People in Learning Organizations discuss their mental models. They challenge their assumptions and strive for personal mastery.
- Third, Learning Organizations are characterized by coordinated action. Everyone works together for continuous improvement. Learning Organizations are characterized by high-involvement philosophies with everyone sharing the power, knowledge, information, and control (Hesselbein, et al, 1996; Kauffman, 1980; Kim, 1994; Kofman & Senge, 1995; Senge, 1990; Vaill, 1996).

A Learning Organization is a non-hierarchical organization where all stakeholders are involved in deciding how the organization will conduct itself. Knowledge, information, power, and control are not held by lone managers; instead leaders develop people. Leaders in a Learning Organization are in charge of establishing the vision and creating the climate and culture. They set the tone. This is the one thing leaders don't give away; the one thing they have complete control over. The entire team learns together and works toward a shared goal. They have the capacity to see and work with the flow of life as a system and work in a coordinated way to improve the big picture.

In his book *The Fifth Discipline: The Art and Practice of the Learning Organization*, Peter Senge defined a Learning Organization as human beings cooperating in dynamical systems that are in a state of continuous adaptation and improvement (1990). He injected into the field of organizational leadership an original and powerful paradigm called "Systems Thinking"—the Fifth Discipline upon which his book is focused.

## Systems Thinking

The child care and youth development professions are human-service fields. Humans are complex. Working with humans involves constantly changing dynamics of communication and relationships. While a factory-style, mechanistic view of organizations may be effective for the fast food industry or the front lines in the military because tasks are simple and routine and standardization is important, the theories that emphasize the importance of human relationships seem to be a more appropriate view for human service professions.

The metaphor of organizations as machines was articulated during a period in history when science was developing and understanding new principles by adopting analytical, reductionist methods. Science was looking at smaller and smaller parts of the whole: the cell, the molecule, the atom. Problem solving in this paradigm involved breaking the machine into components, studying each part in isolation, identifying defective cogs in the machine, and drawing conclusions about the whole.

Peter Senge says that this type of linear and mechanistic thinking is ineffective for leading organizations because most issues are complex and interrelated in ways that defy linear causation.

What are systems? Systems are composed of a group of interrelated parts. "Heaps" are also composed of many parts, but they are not interrelated. A pile of hay is a heap, not a system. If you divide the pile in half, you get two smaller and functionally equivalent piles of hay.

The parts of a system affect each other and function as a whole. When the whole is affected, all parts are affected. When one part is affected, all parts are affected because individual parts are in communication and feedback with each other (Ollhoff & Walcheski, 2002). Ecosystems, legal systems, and the nervous system are examples of systems. A cow is a system. It has many parts that function together to create organs, and organ systems that are parts of the entire organism. If you divide a cow in half, what do you get? Not two cows!

The defining characteristic of a system is that it cannot be understood as a function of its isolated parts. The behavior of the system does not depend on what each part is doing individually, but on how each part is interacting with the other parts. Understanding a system requires understanding how it fits into larger systems of which it is a part. How we define the parts is fundamentally a matter of perspective and purpose, not intrinsic in the nature of the larger system—the real thing we are looking at. (Kofman & Senge, 1993). For example, if we look at a single atom or compound in the body of a cow, how we define it is rather limited if we do not perceive that it combines with other atoms and compounds to create a molecule, and that these molecules come together to form cells, which interrelate with other cells to form organs, which join up with other organs to form organ systems, which all work together systemically to form the whole cow.

Systems thinking is a paradigm premised upon the "primacy of the whole." Seeking to understand the whole dominates over the parts. It "is a way to see the world, looking at wholes and their interactive pieces instead of the individual parts. Systems thinking looks at the dynamics of the entire whole" (Ollhoff & Walcheski, 2002). In order to understand problems and their solutions, linear and mechanistic thinking must give way to non-linear and organic thinking—systems thinking.

Systems thinking views the world we live in as a complicated one and views life's problems as complicated and often chaotic systems in a constant state of change. Systems problem solving looks at the big picture and examines the complexity of the interrelationships of systems involved in the problem and in possible solutions.

At the heart of a Learning Organization is a shift of mind—from seeing ourselves as separate from the world to connected to the world, from seeing problems as caused by someone or something "out there" to seeing how our own actions create the problems we experience. A Learning Organization is a place where people are continually discovering how they create their reality, and how they can change it (Senge, 1990).

Communities, workplace settings, and child care and youth development organizations are all very complex. They contain many systems and subsystems. Environmental factors, staff composition, accounting, human resources, socio-economic factors, professional development, and parent involvement are just a few systems that interrelate in complex ways with other elements in the system.

Running a school-age care or child development agency is not something that can be summed up in a policies and procedures manual because it involves many complex sub-systems. Therefore, child care administrators and caregivers must be trained and educated with the goal of increasing creative leadership, decision making, and problem-solving skills.

Our organization intentionally blurs the lines between the roles of administrators, caregivers, and students. Learning is not something that is only done by students; teaching is not something that is only done by adults. Agency directors, site directors, and caregivers must be role models of not only teaching, but also of learning. The philosophy of our organization as a community of learners is an essential element in a model of a non-hierarchical Learning Organization where all stakeholders are involved in deciding how the organization will conduct itself. Caregivers in many school-age care agencies often complain bitterly about administrative decisions, which interfere with their ability to do their jobs. This is a tragedy.

The current hierarchical system that separates the thinkers (administrators) from the workers (caregivers) is the source of this tragedy. This segregation of power creates a role for caregivers that does not expect them to know a great deal about learning, teaching, organizational management, or child development; which leads to less competent caregivers, which creates a stronger need for administrative control, which leads to even less competent caregivers, and so on.

Our organization, a model of a Learning Organization, is a company in which all employees do whatever needs to be done in order to accomplish our mission, rather than follow narrowly defined job descriptions. An accreditation endorser inspecting our programs once insisted on seeing an organizational chart that described the structure of the organization. After explaining that the organization was non-hierarchical and that knowledge, information, power, and control were dispersed throughout the organization, the endorser still demanded to see an organizational chart. She wanted to see boxes in the shape of a pyramid, but what I eventually produced and showed her was something entirely different.

In most organizations the directors are at the top of the human pyramid and the caregivers are at the bottom, like this.

In our organization the hierarchy of the organization is flipped upside down.

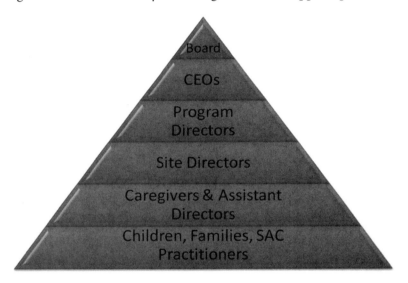

This model resembles a house. The line staff, who work directly with the kids and families, are at the top—the roof, viewed as the most influential and most powerful members of the team. The administrative/managerial staff are viewed as the walls—they support the roof. Support staff work for the line staff, supporting them and getting them the resources they need to accomplish the mission. This house is built on a foundation of our mission, and our values. This isn't to say the support staff in this structure now get paid less. They still have more education, experience, and ultimate responsibility, so the pay structure does not change. Similarly to the employees in the Hawthorne Electric story, we have found our staff to be the most dedicated, hard working, and happy staff we have worked with.

**Power Staff =**

**Top of the Organization**

**Caregivers, Group Leaders, Assistant Directors, & Site Directors:**

Those who facilitate the positive development of children, and create the model of quality.

| Director of Finances & Customer Service Staff: | Youth Program Directors: | Director of Operations: |
|---|---|---|
| Build Capacity | Safety Control | Leadership & Management |
| Payroll | Quality Control | Partnerships |
| Financial Resources | Curriculum Support | Advocacy |
| Fiscal Management | Field Trip Scheduling | Research |
| Accounts Receivable | Mentoring & Guidance to Staff | Resource Development |
| Information | Improvement and Accreditation Assitance | Outreach |
| Budget Forecasting | | Training |

# Foundation of Values

## Story Time: Finding the Pony

Billy and Peter were two children in different homes who both arose on Christmas morning, full of Christmas excitement, eager to unwrap their gifts.

Billy finds a roomful of toys. He rips into them. Wrapping paper flies through the air. In just a few minutes all the presents are unwrapped, but Billy begins to cry because none is the exact toy he wanted.

Peter runs down the stairs only to find the room is almost full with a huge, smelly pile of horse manure. A huge smile breaks out on the child's face and he immediately begins to dig with an unexpected fervor and eagerness. When asked why he is digging, he answers, "With all this manure, there's got to be a pony in here somewhere!" (Kline & Saunders, 1998, p. 78).

Leaders help their constituents develop their strengths and abilities. They find potential in people and develop their potential into actual abilities. Great leaders observe people carefully to discover and acknowledge their potential. They challenge them and help them learn and grow. Sometimes potential strengths are difficult to find, but their weaknesses are glaring, so often bosses focus on weaknesses. Sometimes you need to find the pony within the people you work with, feed that pony, and nurture it into a racehorse.

## Promoting the Positive

*There are souls in this world which have the gift of finding joy everywhere and of leaving it behind them when they go.*
—*Frederick William Faber*

It is important to establish an organizational culture of positive thinking. Everyone in the organization must believe that anyone is capable of anything and that any situation can be improved. The culture must be one that respects people and what they can do, and challenges all members of the organization to be the very best they can be. Respect exists everywhere in the organization, flowing up and down in the power structure. In a Learning Organization, every situation is an opportunity to learn and improve (Kline & Saunders, 1998).

In his landmark book *The Power of Positive Thinking*, Norman Vincent Peale states, "When you expect the best, you release a magnetic force in your mind which by a law of attraction tends to bring the best to you. But if you expect the worst, you release from your mind the power of repulsion which tends to force the best from you. It is amazing how a sustained expectation of the best sets in motion forces which cause the best to materialize" (1952, p. 91).

Effective leaders generate positive energy in others. Leaders create meaning by engaging the emotions of employees. Because learning is an emotional process, the corporate culture is a supportive place to be (Kline & Saunders, 1998). Leaders of Learning Organizations have trust and confidence in their followers. Research shows that followers perform better when their leaders have high expectations of them (Eden, 1990; McNatt, 2000). A team with high expectations, emotional energy, and enthusiasm can provide its members with a positive and rewarding experience that they may never in their lives experience again.

*The Code of Ethics for School-Age Care* states, "We will provide a workplace that is safe, empowering, and emotionally supportive. In a spirit of professional pride and community, we will acknowledge the experience and education of staff as together we respond to the needs of children and youth" (Charron, 2001, p. 10).

## Story Time: Little Bloodsuckers

Years ago we had a terrible mosquito problem, and then someone invented a solution to the problem—DDT, the insecticide. We were told it was safe. A friend of mine remembers riding his bike with friends as the DDT trucks drove through their neighborhood spraying great clouds of DDT. Their game was to try to keep up; to ride fast enough to stay in the DDT clouds.

The use of an insecticide is another example of a diminishing feedback system—a system that negates a change in the system. The system responds to rising numbers of mosquitoes with an insecticide that decreases the number of mosquitoes—a simple, "obvious" solution, but not when you look at the big picture. When you examine the bigger systems, you find that the obvious solution is often a catastrophic failure.

DDT was ingested not only by mosquitoes and little boys on their bikes, but by birds that eat mosquitoes. What we didn't know is that DDT causes the egg shells of birds to be too soft and easily breakable. When birds ingested DDT, their eggs would often break in their nests. DDT killed mosquitoes, but also killed birds that preyed on mosquitoes, which, in the long term, resulted in more mosquitoes. Systems fight back!

The point is that by understanding the interrelationships and complex patterns of systems and subsystems of a child care organization and other human endeavors, people can more adequately think about the problems they face and how to fix them in a long-term way. By looking at individual parts of the problems ("snapshots"), people fail to see how the solutions they choose may only cause additional problems over time, and that the wrong "cures" are often worse than the original disease.

## Story Time: Bunny Love

*Ideas are like rabbits. You get a couple and learn how to handle them, and pretty soon you have a dozen.*
*—John Steinbeck*

Bunnies are prolific. Bunny love is an example of an amplifying feedback system. When two rabbits of the opposite sex get together and do their thing, they may spawn ten new rabbits. When the new batch of rabbits begin making whoopee, before long you have dozens of rabbits, scores of rabbits, hundreds of rabbits. As long as there is an adequate food supply and predators are in short supply the system can crank out an escalating number of rabbits.

In child care organizations, a director might decide to cut costs in order to have more money in the bank (a diminishing feedback system). In doing so, he may create a destructive amplifying feedback system. Cutting certain costs may lead to a lower quality, which may lead to a poor reputation in the community, which may lead to fewer children in the program which leads to less money in the bank, less money for staff training, which leads to a less safe program, which leads to an injury, which results in a law suit, which bankrupts the center. In amplifying feedback systems; the chances of the action in the system happening again is increased.

## Story Time: Popping Popcorn May Cause Seizures

One of the lessons that systems thinking teaches us is that unintended consequences often happen. Systems are interdependent. Consequences often show up in the most vulnerable part of the system. This true story illustrates that lesson. Warning: if you now or have ever worked as a director of a school-age care program sharing school space, and were ever concerned about the relationship with the school faculty, you may find this story painful.

Our school-age child care programs operate in elementary schools using shared space. On one particular Monday, one of our schools was having an in-service training day for the school faculty, with no classes for the day. The school had hired a special presenter, a facilitator flown in from California to lead the in-service learning for the faculty.

For us, this meant we provided a full-day child care program for the many parents who worked on school in-service days. Our child care programs are like a home away from home and the staff are like extended family. It is very homey and we often cook, and eat, and try to do the same things the kids who stay home with their parents do.

This day, the director decided to microwave a batch of popcorn for an informal snack. She left the bag in the microwave a little bit too long. The bag was scorched and a little burned. The microwave got a little smoky. No biggie.

But, the microwave had been rolled out on a cart and plugged in to an outlet located directly beneath the smoke detector.

The school fire alarm went off. The entire school had to be evacuated, even the teachers in the in-service had to leave the building. That would have been plenty bad enough—maybe bad enough to give the director some bad dreams. But as it turned out, the expert trainer and presenter that the school had hired to facilitate the in-service had a seizure disorder. The flashing lights of the fire alarm triggered a seizure, and she had to be taken away in an ambulance. In-service cancelled, game over!

## Self-Awareness and Self-Direction

In order to be able to guide their own learning, exercise power and control, and develop goals, learners must be able to assess themselves. In order to develop personal mastery of their work, people must generate self-evaluation and transformation. Coming to terms with oneself through introspection and change is the preparation for transformational leadership. Only by deeply examining core values and beliefs can paradigm shifts occur and inner growth be achieved.

Learning Organizations need leaders who have successfully navigated deep personal change—leaders who have been through their own transformations—to facilitate the transformation of others (Rolls, 1995). Members of Learning Organizations must be critically reflective practitioners, so leaders must know and teach the process of self-evaluation (Kline & Saunders, 1998).

Adult learning is a process of mental inquiry experienced through life and situations, not a passive reception of content and subjects. Adults have a self-concept and a need of being seen by others as being responsible for their own decisions and capable of self-direction (Knowles, 1998). The philosophy of a Learning Organization recognizes this and acknowledges that adults learn best when they are committed to taking charge of their own learning. Successful leaders are especially self-directed. They know themselves, have a clear role and purpose, have high standards, and have ambitious goals.

Effective organizational leaders are independent and autonomous, but they also know that the learning and understanding gained through relationships with other people are the keys to self-direction. This paradox of self-direction and learning from others is resolved by understanding that leaders learn from others, but are not made by others. The self and the others are synthesized through self-invention (Bennis, 1994). Lifelong learners enthusiastically solicit knowledge, opinions, and ideas from other people. "They don't make the assumption that they know it all or that most other people have little to contribute. Just the opposite, they believe that with the right approach, they can learn from anyone under almost any circumstance" (Kotter, 1996, p. 182).

A primary lesson of self-knowledge is, "You are your own best teacher." Successful leaders have to teach themselves. They reach a point in life where they see learning as something intimately connected with themselves. They know they have to learn new things, driven by hunger for knowledge and their own perception of the gap between what they are and what they want to be (Bennis, 1994). The values of a leader are strengthened by and often derived from a deeper self-knowledge. Through introspectively delving deeper, leaders generate an ongoing opportunity to change reality—a continuous learning opportunity.

## Try This: Self-Awareness Exercise

An effective leader needs self-awareness. Make a list of your strengths and weaknesses. Now make a list of what you think your staff may think are your strengths and weaknesses. How different is this list? If you are really brave, ask your staff to list your strengths and weaknesses. How do their lists compare to yours?

## Mistakes

*Failure is the foundation of success, and the means by which it is achieved.*
*—Lao Tsu*

*Recently, I was asked if I was going to fire an employee who made a mistake that cost the company $600,000. No, I replied, I just spent $600,000 training him. Why would I want somebody to hire his experience?*
*—Thomas J. Watson*

In Learning Organizations mistakes are accepted and expected. Leaders of organizations must continuously learn and constantly reinvent themselves. Learning Organization leaders learn from their mistakes and experiences. Learning Organization leaders take risks, make mistakes, and gain satisfaction from the lessons they learn. They see learning not as a confession of ignorance, but as a way of being. Lead learners must view mistakes as steppingstones to continuous learning, and essential to further business growth (Kline & Saunders, 1998). If mistakes are not being made, new possibilities are being ignored. The world's greatest advances and discoveries were the result of mistakes. Members of Learning Organizations learn from their mistakes, learn to take responsibility for them, and learn not to repeat them. Thomas Edison once said, "I have not failed. I've just found ten thousand ways that won't work."

An effective leader must be big enough to admit his mistakes, smart enough to profit from them, and strong enough to correct them. Anyone who refuses to profit by his mistakes is a fool. Every mistake is an opportunity to increase competency.

Chelsea has a story about the value hidden within mistakes. Here is her story. A few years back, a site director of ours made one of the worst mistakes someone can make in our field: she left a five-year-old at a field trip site, violating one of our very few strict procedures.

She called me as the bus was about to arrive at her site to inform me that she had just realized this child was missing. I raced to pick the child up and met my site director and the child's angry parents in the parking lot of our school. By the time the parents left, the site director was in tears. I looked at her and just said, "Meet me at 9:30 in my office tomorrow morning."

I was not sure what I was going to do. The obvious solution was to fire her. Most supervisors would not have questioned this. At 9:30 the next day, she was in my office with a stack of papers. She had stayed up most of the night writing down how she had left the child back. She also had spent most of the night writing down all the ways she would never let that happen again if allowed to keep her job. We talked extensively about what happened and how she planned to prevent this from happening in the future. She had analyzed the situation well. I let her stay and here's why.

Because of that mistake, I could practically guarantee that no child from that site would ever get left behind on a field trip as long as that site director was in charge. Not only could I make that guarantee, but that site director stood up at every new-hire orientation for the next three years and told that story (usually in tears) when we got to the field trip procedures. By accepting that mistake and learning from it, we gained more than we could have by firing her and hiring a brand new site director who could just as easily make the same mistake.

People say, "Success always takes place in private, and failure in the full view of others." I say, "If at first you don't succeed, destroy all evidence that you tried!" My daughter says, "If at first you don't succeed, get new batteries."

## Story Time: Tragedy of the Commons
In our organization, we have ten child care directors who each lead a school-based program. We have a central office space and common area where they store

common supplies used in their programs: snack, art, science, curriculum books, etc. Every director wants his or her program to be the highest quality possible. All of the directors are committed to the children, families, and key stakeholders in their program. At one point in our history, when supplies were purchased, each director would take the best of the supplies back to his site. They would take more than their share, so that they could provide the best quality possible. When a great employment application came in, the directors would compete to hire that person. This created a win-lose situation. The director who got to the resources first and took more than his or her share would win and the one who got to them last would lose. This created competition and destroyed reciprocity. It created systems of competition, and in the end everyone lost. Systems thinkers refer to this complex, interrelated system archetype as the "Tragedy of the Commons." It is also called "sub-optimizing." When we learned about systems and focused on the big picture, staff began to understand the relevancy of conservation to the organization as a whole and found meaning in reciprocity and sacrifice to their own programs.

## Try This: Stakeholder Analysis

Who are your stakeholders? A stakeholder is any person, group, or organization that utilizes an organization's resources, attention, or output, or is affected by its output. Examples of the stakeholders of child care and youth development organizations might include: the children and families, third-party payers such as the state's Children, Youth, and Families Departments, employees, the board of directors, volunteers, school staff and faculties, other allied nonprofit organizations, and even the banks and vendors utilized by the organization. Attention to stakeholder concerns is crucial. The key to success for nonprofit organizations is the satisfaction of key stakeholders. It is also an ethical necessity since only by understanding stakeholder interests and concerns is an organization likely to take truly ethical action (Bryson, 1995).

Conduct a stakeholder analysis. Effective leaders should define the mission and the values of their organization or program in relation to key stakeholders. Specifically identify, by name, who your organization's internal and external stakeholders are, how they evaluate the organization, how they influence the organization, what the organization needs and receives from them, and how important they are. Articulate a statement of the values that address how the organization conducts its business and how it wants to treat the key stakeholders. Put yourself and your team in the shoes of others, especially external stakeholders, then your organization or program can make a dispassionate assessment of the organizations performance and articulate a set of values (Bryson, 1995; Bryson & Alston, 1996).

## Bringing It Home

The evolution of our leadership theories began when we worked for a large hierarchical organization, focused on creating profit. When we founded our new organization, we experienced a profound "Galilean" paradigm shift. Galileo moved us from looking at the earth as the center around which all else revolved to seeing our place in a broader system (Kofman & Senge, 1995). We broke away from the status quo. Through generative learning, we developed a new vision, new goals, and new uncompromising values. We had a vision, not just to create an agency that offered premier, top-quality school-age care, but to create an agency that shared and taught the strategies and methods used to create this level of quality with other providers—the "competitors."

The organization was founded on the basic belief in doing what is in the best interest of children—all children. We would not be governed by greed and fear, but by a commitment to the long-term picture of the greater society. The goal of the organization is to be a model of world-class quality, a premier example of quality standards, to see healthier children, healthier families, and a healthier community.

We shifted the focus from fiscal management to quality improvement. We shifted the organizational paradigms from control to empowerment, from busyness to playfulness, from activity-driven to community-building. We focused on the big picture and the powerful amplifying feedback systems and subsystems of quality that affected fiscal management. We invested in staff salary increases and professional development. We invested in top-quality supplies and equipment. We raised quality standards. Staff morale, customer satisfaction, and financial surpluses increased. Investing in quality improvement created systems that had a positive impact on the bottom line.

We shifted from a paradigm of control to one of empowerment. Under the new paradigm, we squashed the hierarchy and gave employees at all levels the knowledge and information needed to exercise power and control. Subsidiarity means giving away power. It is at the heart of a Learning Organization where power is given to those who are closest to the action (Handy, 1995). We blurred the lines between the roles of administrators and caregivers. Caregivers are highly trained and can be trusted to make decisions and guide the development of the program and the organization.

We value and appreciate the importance of the caregivers. We invest in them massively and trust them completely. They are expected to make mistakes and to learn from their mistakes. It is important to us that all employees enjoy their jobs and find their work meaningful. Caregivers are expected to be playful and have fun. "Learning often occurs best through 'play,' through interactions in a transitional medium where it is safe to experiment and reflect" (Koffman & Senge, 1995, p. 36).

Trust and playfulness are strong parts of the culture of the organization. Trust facilitates an assumption of competence—that each individual can be expected to perform to the limit of his or her competence, with the minimum of supervision (Handy, 1995). "The culture dictates the ways in which members of that organization relate to one another" (Kline & Saunders, 1998, p. 24). The culture of an organization creates cycles of causality, an understanding of which allows leaders to see how they can identify and change the patterns that control events and outcomes.

We understand that people who enjoy their work and find it meaningful are more productive, more committed, and do a better job. Organizational change is hard work, "But it can ultimately be more satisfying work if we make it fun. And the clue to making it fun is putting people in charge of the change rather than imposing the change from the top" (Kanter, 1995, p. 83). A playful and fun-filled work environment creates better staff teams. This results in a higher-quality program, which results in healthier and happier families, which in the long term is good business sense.

Organizational leaders can be transformational leaders with an understanding of systems thinking. By understanding the interrelationships and complex patterns of the systems and subsystems of business and other human endeavors, leaders can more adequately think about the problems they face and how to fix them in a long-term way. By trusting and empowering staff, looking out for their best interest, and genuinely caring about their emotional well-being, leaders can develop more productive and effective staff teams.

When leaders create healthy and positive work environments and a culture of playfulness they can thereby increase job satisfaction and performance. "People who know that their company cares about them will come to care more and more about their company and will want to give their best to it. They'll want to assess their own actions so they can improve their performance" (Kline & Saunders, 1998, p. 44). Leaders can focus on the big picture and the powerful amplifying feedback systems that can strengthen and transform their organizations.

Systems can be powerful; they can drive change and growth even when we are unaware of their existence. One of the lessons that systems thinking teaches us is that cause and effect may not be closely related in time and space. The way our organization grows and prospers illustrates that lesson, as told in the story below. The story also shows that although investing in quality might require an initial financial sacrifice, the investment definitely pays off.

When we broke away from that dysfunctional organization and founded our new organization, we created some amplifying feedback systems. We invested in quality. We paid staff more; we purchased more and better supplies and equipment; we served healthier (more expensive) food; we invested in staff training. We didn't invest in quality because we were wealthy. We didn't do it because we were reckless fiscal managers. We did it because we knew we were creating amplifying feedback systems. We knew that if we invested in quality it would result in escalating quality improvement. Parents recognized this increase in quality, word-of-mouth spread the good news, and more parents enrolled their children, so we had more funds to work with. We invested these funds in further improving quality. Children were happier and better behaved, which lead to happier staff, so turnover was low and we spent less time and money on recruitment and orienting new staff. We invested these savings on better staff training, which resulted in higher quality and a safer program, which resulted in lower insurance rates.

When a coach at our first school was transferred to a new school and promoted to assistant principal, she acknowledged our high quality by asking us to start a new program at her new school. Our budget doubled overnight. We invested this increase in quality systems. We became the first nationally accredited school-based program in the country. Our reputation for quality grew.

A parent whose child attended our first school moved and transferred her child to another school. She noticed that the program there was of much lower quality than ours, so she contacted the principal. Together they visited one of our programs. The principal noticed a dramatic difference in quality and asked us to open up a new program at her school. Our budget grew and again we invested in quality. This principal told her best friend (who was also a principal) about our program. The friend asked us to start a program at her school. Again we invested in quality.

The coach who was promoted to assistant principal was promoted to principal and transferred to a new school. The first thing she did was request that we bring a program to her new school. Bigger budget—invested in staff raises, staff training, and quality programming.

The nurse at our very first school transferred to a newly constructed school. The day the principal was selected the nurse told her that she had to recruit us to provide a program. Every single program we have started can be traced to the word-of-mouth and reputation for quality that were created by these systems. Our first year (1998) we had an annual budget of $60,000; our 2011 annual budget is $1,750,000. To date we have declined to provide child care at thirteen schools that have requested our services. We only state this to point out that our annual budget to date could have easily exceeded four million dollars, but we have intentionally limited our growth so that we guarantee high quality. Creating a Learning Organization that understands systems is a proven recipe for success.

## Story Time: The Fox and the Hedgehog

The fox knows many things, but the hedgehog knows one big thing. The fox is a cunning creature, able to devise a myriad of complex strategies for sneak attacks upon the hedgehog. Day in and day out, the fox circles around the hedgehog's den, waiting for the perfect moment to pounce. Fast, sleek, beautiful, fleet of foot, and crafty, the fox looks like the sure winner. The hedgehog, on the other hand, is a dreary creature, looking like a genetic mix-up between a porcupine and a small armadillo. He waddles along, going about his simple day, searching for lunch and taking care of his home. The fox waits in cunning silence at the juncture in the trail. The hedgehog, minding his own business, wanders right into the path of the fox. "Aha, I've got you now!" Thinks the fox. He leaps out, bounding across the ground, lightning fast. The little hedgehog, sensing danger, looks up and thinks, "Here we go again. Will he ever learn?" Rolling up into a little ball, the hedgehog becomes a sphere of sharp spikes, pointing outward in all directions. The fox, bounding toward his prey, sees the hedgehog defense and calls off the attack. Retreating back to the forest, the fox begins to calculate a new line of attack. Each day, some version of this battle between the hedgehog and the fox takes place, and despite the greater cunning of the fox, the hedgehog always wins.

People are either like foxes or hedgehogs. Foxes pursue many ends at the same time and see the world in all its complexity. They are distracted and diffused moving on many levels at once, never integrating their thinking into one overall concept or unifying vision. Hedgehogs simplify a complex world into a single organizing idea, a basic principle or concept that unifies and guides everything; a high-quality principle. Hedgehogs are not stupid. Einstein was a hedgehog. He understood that the essence of profound insight is simplicity. What could be more simple than $E=mc2$? (Collins, 2001). Our hedgehog idea is simple. Invest in quality. Quality does not cost; quality pays!

## Conclusion

The point is that creating systems of quality and continuous quality improvement does not COST. In financial terms, INVESTING IN QUALITY PAYS! Create systems that drive quality improvement, customer service, the development of competencies, and continuous learning. Create systems in the environments,

84

relationships, and experiences that propel innovation and creative problem solving. Create systems that fuel teamwork, attention to detail, and accountability. Create systems that engage emotions and develop leadership skills in people.

## Discussion Questions

1. Who are your customers? Who needs what you provide?

2. When the people who work directly with the children in your organization have more knowledge and information, when they have more power and control over problem solving, decision making, and program development, what effects can you predict? How will this affect your customer service? What systems does this set in motion?

3. What systemic changes can you predict when you invest in organization-wide professional development? What will staff learning lead to? What systems does this set in motion?

## Helpful Resources

Must Reads: *Stepping in Wholes: An Introduction to Complex Systems*, by Jim Ollhoff and Michael Malcheski; and *Once Upon a Complex Time: Using Stories to Understand Systems*, by Richard Brynteson. Purchase both at www.sparrowmediagroup.com

*The Fifth Discipline: the Art and Practice of a Learning Organization* by Peter Senge (2006), Doubleday Publishing.

## Reference Notes

Berlin, I. (1993). The hedgehog and the fox. Chicago: Elephant Paperbacks.

DiBella, A. (2001). *Learning practices: Assessment and action for organizational improvement*. Upper Saddle River, NJ: Prentice Hall.

Eden, D. (1990). *Pygmalion in management: Productivity as a self-fulfilling prophecy*. Lexington, MA: Lexington Books.

Gardner, H. (1993). *Multiple intelligences: the theory in practice.* New York: Basic Books.

Kanter, R. (1995). Mastering change. In S. Chawla & J. Renesch (Eds.), *Learning Organizations* (p. 11–45). Portland, OR: Productivity Press.

Kline, P., & Saunders, B. (1998). *Ten steps to a learning organization.* Arlington, VA: Great Ocean Publishers.

Knowles, M. (1998). *The adult learner: The definitive classic in adult education and human resource development.* Woburn, MA: Butterworth-Heinemann.

Kofman, F., Senge, P. M. (1995). Communities of commitment: The heart of learning organizations. In S. Chawla & J. Renesch (Eds.), *Learning Organizations* (p. 11–45). Portland, OR: Productivity Press.

Kouzes, J. & Posner, B. (1995). *The leadership challenge: How to keep getting extraordinary things done in organizations.* San Francisco: Jossey-Bass, Inc.

Marshall, L., Mobley, S., & Calvert, G. (1995). Why smart organizations don't learn.. In S. Chawla & J. Renesch (Eds.), *Learning Organizations* (p. 111–125). Portland, OR: Productivity Press.

McNatt, D. B. (2000). Ancient Pygmalion joins contemporary management: A meta-analysis of the result. *Journal of Applied Psychology*, 85, 314–322.

Morgan, G. (1997). *Images of Organization.* Thousand Oaks, CA: Sage Publications, Inc.

Osland, J., Kolb, D., & Rubin, I. (2001). *Organizational behavior: An experiential approach.* Upper Saddle River, NJ: Prentice Hall.

Peale, N. (1952). *The power of positive thinking.* New York: Prentice-Hall, Inc.

Pollard, W. (1996). The leader who serves. In Hesselbein, F., Goldsmith, M., & Beckhard, R. (Eds.). *The leader of the future.* San Francisco: Jossey-Bass Publishers.

Rolls, J. (1995). The transformational leader: The wellspring of the learning organization. In S. Chawla & J. Renesch (Eds.), *Learning Organizations* (p. 101–108). Portland, OR: Productivity Press.

Yukl, G. (2002). *Leadership in organizations.* Upper Saddle River, NJ: Prentice Hall.

# Chapter 5: Learning for Life

*Learning is like rowing upstream; not to advance is to drop back.*
*—Chinese proverb*

*Who dares to teach must never cease to learn.*
*—John Cotton Dana*

## Introduction

*Education is the best provision for old age.*
*—Aristotle*

*Don't fear the reaper.*
*—Blue Öyster Cult*

Do you want to have a long life? Do you want to keep your wits if you have the fortune to see old age? Would you like to avoid the mental decline that can accompany old age? We know that people who keep learning as they get older live longer. We know that lifelong learners retain their wit in old age. Lifelong learners have less occurrence of Alzheimer's disease. Lifelong learners live longer and live smarter than those who do not intentionally strive for continuous learning.

We're planning on living FOREVER! So far, so good!

Effective leadership is not learned; effective leadership is learning. The one attribute that a leader must possess in order to develop an organization's human capital is lifelong learning. An organizational leader must act as the lead learner of the organization. The leader of an organization must be a teacher, mentor, coach, and a facilitator of learning. Continuous learning is a paramount task that an effective leader needs to engage in as an ongoing process in the job (Vaill, 1996).

The key for total leaders is to provide useful learning experiences for themselves and their staffs and to establish clear and compelling ways for the organization to benefit from what everyone learns (Schwahn & Spady, 1998). Developing tactics for planning and decision making based on new learning is essential to personal and organizational well-being and success. The most important and most essential trait of a leader is to be a lifetime learner and the lead learner of the organization.

We have coined the phrase "sponginess" when looking for new staff. Sponginess is important at all levels of our organization, but is crucial for a site director applicant. We would rather hire a person who may be very "green" but extremely willing to learn and train him or her to have the "how to do it" skills than hire an "old dog" who "knows everything there is to know about this field."

When we interview someone who has less experience and knowledge than we desire, we typically say, "Okay, she lacks some of the skills we want, but is she spongy?" The most important trait for us is the ability to learn. Is she an "old dog" that shows resistance to learning new tricks or is she like a sponge, greedy to soak up and apply new information? Our reasoning is that technical skills are easier to acquire than a teamwork and service attitude.

Effective leaders must be committed examples of lifelong learners—sponges for learning opportunities in every situation. Chelsea has a story that illustrates this. Here is her story. I have always worked with children. All of my education has been centered on children. I have never taken business or accounting courses. Yet I find myself the financial director of our organization—scary huh? A few years ago, I got a notice that the Department of Labor was conducting an audit of our payroll records. Now, under the circumstances, I was a little nervous. As we have created and developed this organization, I have always learned by doing—the trial and error method. A labor audit seemed about as much fun as an enema of battery acid.

I had to work hard to find the pony in this situation, but I did. I chose to view this situation as an opportunity for free learning. I figured that if I asked enough questions during the audit that I would not only be able to fix any mistakes I had made, but I would learn enough to prevent any errors in the future. This turned out to be exactly what happened. I had made a few mistakes, but I was able to learn what I had been doing wrong, fix the problems, and figure out how to never repeat them. We were fined a little more than $150. While this was not the free training I had hoped for, this was the cheapest accounting training I could have asked for!

Take the sponge test. Are you a "sponge," a voracious learner attending every training event and reading everything you can get your hands on? Reading this book is a good sign that you might be. List other learning opportunities you have taken advantage of in the last six months.

## Critical Reflection

Successful leaders are critically reflective practitioners. They apply the rewards from their continuous quest for knowledge to their daily practices. Self-reflection is fundamental to becoming an effective leader. One of the mental habits that support lifelong learning is humble self-reflection, honest assessment of successes and failures (Kotter, 1996).

Effective leaders must learn in broad, systemic ways that go far beyond the simple "how-to" lists marketed as "five simple strategies to lead an organization" or "seven keys to success." Our leadership theory recognizes that organizations and humans are too complex and solutions and effective actions are too complicated for simplistic, one-size-fits-all strategies.

The changing needs of childhood, families, education and society cause increased anxiety because we must rapidly learn new skills. Reinventing ourselves is a lifelong and continuous learning process. Organizational leaders must continually drive their ambition for new learning, and continually apply this new learning in practical ways to develop the human capital of their organizations.

## Organizational Learning

Not surprisingly, learning is an integral part of a Learning Organization. Learning gets to the heart of what it means to be human. Through learning we re-create ourselves, and become able to do things we not were able to do before. Through learning we re-perceive the world and our relationship to it. Through learning we extend our capacity to create, and to be part of the generative process of life (Senge, 1990). Senge's definition of team learning is "the process of aligning and developing the capacity of a team to create the results its members truly desire. It builds on personal mastery, for talented teams are made up of talented individuals" (1990, p. 236).

The culture of learning that exists in any organization has a profound impact on performance. If learning is something that happens at a mandatory training event once every six months, the effect is very different than in an organization where every opportunity to learn is taken advantage of at every level in the organization. When the entire organization is bathed in a desire for learning, the whole of all organizational learning is far greater than the sum of its parts because powerful learning systems are created that pervade all aspects of the organization and drive innovation. Organizational learning can be categorized as either adaptive learning or generative learning.

Adaptive learning involves the detection and correction of error without any paradigm shift. Adaptive learning involves looking for another solution or strategy that will be successful within the existing mental model. Existing paradigms about values, goals, rules, cultures, plans, and philosophies are operationalized rather than questioned. People attempt to identify and correct errors in a way that maintains the central features of their "Theory in Use." Adaptive learning works on diminishing feedback systems, like a thermostat. It adapts to the environment by turning something on or off. An agricultural example of adaptive learning is a farmer who, when finding insects in his crops, changes the brand of pesticide he is using, or applies the pesticide to the plants more often. In child care a director who finds his employees aren't motivated enough might initiate a token reward system (e.g., give them a special parking space, or gift certificate). A director who finds a student is not meeting academic yearly progress might implement a remediation program (e.g., extended homework time).

Generative learning is an alternative response, which questions the existing variables themselves and subjects them to critical examination. Generative learning leads to a modification in the governing variables themselves. It shifts mental models by which strategies and consequences are framed. Generative learning resolves incompatible organizational paradigms by forming new philosophies and setting new priorities. Generative learning works on amplifying feedback systems. It involves a change in philosophy.

An example of generative learning is that farmer who finds insects in his crops and instead of using his long-used strategy of applying a broad-spectrum pesticide, looks deeper into the complex ecosystems of his farming environment. He generates new strategies based on new philosophies. He may utilize beneficial insects to prey on destructive insects, or use companion plants to repel unwanted insects, or use organic soaps or oils that make plants unattractive to destructive insects while allowing beneficial insects to live, or enhance the soil so that plants become strong enough to resist insects.

In child care a director who finds his employees aren't motivated might seek to discover the big picture and ask them about the causes and reasons for their lack of motivation, or plan a fun teambuilding retreat, or might help them to see how their enthusiasm benefits the lives of the children, or might give them the responsibility for building morale and the power to make changes in the work climate. A director who finds that a child is not making academic yearly progress might learn what has changed in the child's life that might have contributed to this lack of progress, or might learn what teaching methods are being used in the classroom and try another method, or might create field trips and enrichment curriculum that are aligned with the academic standards the child is struggling with, or might help the child to see the relevancy in the need to learn the skill he is lacking.

Adaptive learning is about coping; generative learning is about creating. Adaptive learning looks at the issue at hand; generative learning looks at the big picture. Adaptive learning focuses on solving problems; generative learning focuses on trends of change. Adaptive learning involves looking at the symptoms; generative learning involves looking at the core causes of problems. Adaptive learning focuses on doing what the customer wants; generative learning focuses on creating new things that the customers might truly value, but have never experienced before.

Systems thinking helps to facilitate generative learning and overcome some established mental models. People have mental models or paradigms about how things are and how to behave in certain situations. Mental models are almost unconscious paradigms that affect the way people behave, think, plan, execute, and assess their behavior. They are similar to prejudices. Mental models are reflected in their actual day-to-day practices. These daily practices may be very different than what one would expect to follow from their "Espoused Theory." For example, a child care director might espouse a theory of play-based learning, but rely on the use of worksheets and dittos because of her mental model of the way learning happens in a classroom. A leader may espouse a theory of informing and developing staff, but withhold information from staff about the budget because of his mental model about a director's individual responsibility over the budget and fiscal management.

Learning in and of itself, and not its effect on productivity, is valuable because no one can predict what benefits may result from the learning process. Our organization is a community of learners. Learning is not a process, but a way of being. Leaders must celebrate the learning process for its own sake, not just its end product (Kline & Saunders, 1998). Leaders must also celebrate all learners in the organization equally. Everyone in an organization may not have the same knowledge or talent or learn at the same rate, but every learning experience is valuable and worthy of appreciation (Kline & Saunders, 1998).

### Try This: Lessons Learned Sessions
*It's not whether you get knocked down. It's whether you get up again.*
*—Vince Lombardi*

Conduct "Lessons Learned Sessions." These sessions have become part of the culture of our organization. Earlier we described our philosophy of making mistakes; that they are a valuable part of learning. This is only true if we actually learn by our mistakes. If you create an organizational culture that punishes mistakes, it in effect rewards people for lying and hiding their mistakes, which inhibits organizational learning. In our organization, we learn as a team. We learn from our mistakes as a team.

When an individual or a team in our organization makes a mistake they are expected to bring it up in generative conversation—to put it "on the table." We talk about it as a team and discuss possible strategies that would have prevented the mistake. We record our lessons learned and refer to them the next time a similar situation or event occurs.

## Horizontal Learning

In effective teams, members teach each other by coming together and sharing information. They coach and confront each other appropriately. They engage in creative and effective problem solving, seek and implement program improvements, hold each other accountable for high standards, honor commitments made to each other, and generate win-win solutions to issues. In our organization, this occurs constantly. Leaders must facilitate the transfer of knowledge and power from person to person as much as possible (Kline & Saunders, 1998).

Learners must be able to see personal meaning and relevancy in new learning. According to Malcolm Knowles, "Adults need to know why they need to learn something before undertaking to learn it" (1998, p. 64). Adult learners must be empowered to learn and make practical applications to their learning. All learning must be anchored to authentic tasks or problems. Information can be made available and approached flexibly in a variety of ways for a variety of learning styles. Leaders must encourage and teach learners to structure their own learning, rather than structuring it for them (Kline & Saunders, 1998).

## Cross-Functional Learning

Organizations are composed of many systems. These systems interrelate with each other. Changes in one system may have consequences in other systems. It is difficult to predict how information or skills in one system or field may be important to another area of the organization. The most effective leaders are generalists, knowing and learning a little bit about a lot of things—enough of different disciplines and functions to be able to mediate among them. It is important that leaders stay up-to-date in their field, measure their breadth of knowledge, and add to it continuously.

Cross-functional learning opportunities can help people to connect with different fields of knowledge, so that people understand the functions of others whose jobs are different, but of related importance. Organizational leaders can give people the opportunity to grow and change horizontally and vertically in the company, accessing a variety of work and learning experiences. It is important for organizational leaders to cultivate each employee's abilities in all fields of knowledge, and spread the idea that nothing is forever inaccessible to people (Kline & Saunders, 1998).

Learning should be logical, moral, and fun. "If we do not pay attention to the kind of satisfaction people gain from their work, that they find it pleasurable and enjoyable, we are not going to find people to staff the new organization, because the challenges of change are too overwhelming" (Kanter, 1995, p. 83). Psychologist David E. Berlew, believes that what really excites people and generates enthusiasm are these value-related opportunities—the chance to be tested, to make it on one's own, to take part in a social experiment, to do something well, to do something good, and to change the way things are (Kouzes & Posner, 1995). Followers want to be a part of something significant, and for their work to have real meaning and relevancy.

## Bringing it Home
*Educated men are as much superior to uneducated men as the living are to the dead.*
*—Aristotle*

The Constructivist Learning Theory (stop and say that phrase out loud— Constructivist Learning Theory—didn't you sound smart when you said that!) is similar to the progressive philosophy and the discovery approach to learning, which has surfaced periodically since Dewey in 1938 (Cobb, 1999). Constructivism views learning as a creative rather than a receptive act that involves construction of new meanings by learners within the context of their current knowledge, previous experiences, and social environment. Constructivism capitalizes on social context and social activity to teach children and staff members how to develop self-discipline and a sense of community (Bloom, et al, 1999). Piaget presented Constructivism in 1950 (Smith, 1999), and nowadays it regularly appears in teachers' manuals, curriculum frameworks, educational journals, and education reform literature.

Constructivism is consistent with quality early childhood education and quality school-age care theory due to its focus on the role and perspective of the learner, its focus on the whole learner and the big picture, its acceptance of the social context of the learning environment, its focus on active/hands on learning, its expectations of self-discipline, and its view of schools as caring places (Bloom, et al, 1999; Brooks & Brooks, 1999; Jenlink, et al, 1999; Scherer, 1999). Many traditional classrooms appear to operate on a different mental model where learning is viewed as a one-way flow of information—the teacher opens up the minds of students and pours information in. But in a quality child care learning environment children are allowed to construct their own knowledge by exploring and experimenting with learning materials in playful, social, and meaningful ways.

## Try This: Leadership Book Club

Assign books about relevant topics and discuss them at meetings. Our leadership team is always working on a book as a team. We meet every Monday morning. The only standing item on our agenda is to discuss the book we are reading. Each week we are responsible for reading a couple of chapters and preparing ourselves to discuss the applications to our work at the Monday meeting.

## Try This: Bring the Learning to You

In most organizations, staff are trained by their leaders, which is great. In addition, bringing in outside expertise can be even more effective. Sending a few directors or teachers to a national conference or training event is very wise and very rewarding, and also very expensive. Add up the cost of sending just a few people: registration fee, airfare, hotel, ground transport, food. You can easily bring a nationally recognized trainer right to your organization to work directly with ALL of your staff. Get more bang for your training buck. Bring great trainers directly to your organization and create team learning experiences.

## Conclusion

In our organization, everyone learns as a team. If you lead a child care or youth development organization, the team includes the children. In our organization, the leader's job is not to teach those below him on the human pyramid who are supposed to teach those below them and so on. A leader's job is to be the lead learner, yes, but everyone in the organization—directors, teachers, caregivers, and children—are expected to be leaders and learners and to share the knowledge and information they learn and include and empower those they interact with as they apply their learning to their day-to-day practices.

Continuous learning is an expectation in today's organizations and affords all leaders with endless opportunities to be proactive rather than reactive (Anderson, 1995). Lifelong learning is important to the success of emerging and veteran leaders. "The act of committing oneself to being a lifelong learner can take place at any point on our life" (Bennis & Goldsmith, 1997, p. 8). Are you a lifelong learner? If not, commit to become one today.

## Discussion Questions

1. How do you actively take on the role of the lead learner? Do you take the time you need to be your best self, to be the best educator you can be?

2. Do you rely on worksheets and dittos? Why? Can you think of more creative, constructivist strategies that will help children learn through play?

3. Think about how much learning happens in your organization. How often are training events? How often are mistakes discussed? Does staff learn from mistakes? Are they willing to discuss their mistakes with others?

## Helpful Resources

Download many free workshop handouts with LOTS of meaningful information at
www.childrens-choice.org

## Reference Notes

Bloom, L. A., Perlmutter, J., & Burrell, L. (1999). The general educator: applying constructivism to inclusive classrooms. *Intervention in School and Clinic*, 34, 132–147.

Brooks, M. & Brooks, J. G. (1999). The courage to be constructivist. *Educational Leadership*, 57, 18–24.

Cobb, T. (1999). Applying constructivism: a test for the learner-as-scientist. *Educational Technology, Research and Development*, 47, 15–33.

Covey, S. . *Seven habits of highly effective people.*

Gardner, H. (1993). *Multiple intelligences: the theory in practice.* New York: Basic Books.

Jenlink, P. M., & Kinnucan-Welsch, K. (1999). Learning ways of caring, learning ways of knowing through communities of professional development. *Journal for just and caring education*, 5, 367–385.

Kanter, R. (1995). Mastering change. In S. Chawla & J. Renesch (Eds.), *Learning Organizations* (p. 11–45). Portland, OR: Productivity Press.

Kline, P., & Saunders, B. (1998). *Ten steps to a learning organization.* Arlington, VA: Great Ocean Publishers.

Knowles, M., Holton, E., & Swanson, R. (1998). *The adult learner.* Houston, TX: Gulf Publishing Company.

Osland, J., Kolb, D., & Rubin, I. (2001). *Organizational behavior: An experiential approach.* Upper Saddle River, NJ: Prentice Hall.

Scherer, M. (1999). Perspectives: the C word. *Educational Leadership*, 57, 5–7.

Schwahn, C. & Spady, W. (1998). *Total leaders: Applying the best future-focused change strategies to education.* Arlington, VA: American Association of School Administrators. San Francisco, CA: Jossey-Bass Publishers.

Senge, P. M. (1990). *The fifth discipline: The art and practice of the learning organization.* New York, NY: Doubleday.

Vaill, P. (1996). *Learning as a way of being: Strategies for survival in a world of permanent white water.* San Francisco, CA: Jossey-Bass Publishers.

# Chapter 6: Giving Super Powers

*A leader is best when people barely know he exists. Not so good when people obey and acclaim him. Worse when they despise him. But of a good leader who talks little when his work is done, and his aim fulfilled they will say, "We did it ourselves."*
—Lao Tsu

*Being powerful is like being a lady. If you have to tell people you are, you aren't.*
—Margaret Thatcher

*I've got the power!*
—C&C Music Factory

## Introduction
*If you tell people where to go, but not how to get there,*
*you'll be amazed at the results.*
—General George S. Patton

A substantial and rapidly expanding body of evidence indicates a strong connection between how organizations manage their people and their economic results. Research shows that substantial economic gains of approximately 40 percent can be obtained by implementing high-involvement, empowering management practices (Pheffer, 1998). According to an award-winning study of the high-performance work practices of 968 firms representing all major industries, a one standard deviation increase in use of such practices is associated with a 7 percent decrease in turnover and an $18,000 increase in profits per employee. That's right, PER EMPLOYEE, and subsequent studies have found even larger economic benefits (Huselid, 1995). Now, you may be thinking, "Wait, we are a nonprofit organization. Our mission is not about making a profit, but caring for children." If you are thinking that, you are neglecting the first rule of leadership in a not-for-profit organization: No Money = No Mission.

How does this happen? It is simple—people work harder because of the increased involvement and commitment that comes from having more control and input in their work. People work harder when they are encouraged to build skills and competence; they work more responsibly when more responsibility is placed in their hands. Stephen Covey says, "An empowered organization is one in which individuals have the knowledge, skill, desire, and opportunity to personally succeed in a way that leads to collective organizational success." Ken Blanchard says, "People already have power through their knowledge and motivation. Empowerment is letting this power out!"

Remember Frederick Taylor and Pouring Foundations from chapter 2? He was the mean-sounding guy who viewed employees as automatons and was fond of telling his workers, "You are not supposed to think. There are other people paid for thinking around here." Today's managers still operating under the command-and-control paradigm conceive of their job as making decisions, giving orders, and ensuring that subordinates obey. People in these types of organizations speak in terms of "we and they," or workers against managers. Unfortunately, management practices in many organizations are firmly grounded in this hierarchical mental model, and in many more practices are moving toward and not away from this paradigm, even while a growing body of evidence shows this to be ineffective and even contrary to the best interests of the organizations.

After graduating from the New Mexico Military Institute, Mike's first job was as a supervisor of a school-age child care program. This is his story. My leadership courses there completely embedded a paradigm of top-down control in my mind. At NMMI, I was a troop commander. I had more than sixty cadets under my command. I had taken several leadership courses and had learned a lot about leadership. I considered myself a pretty good leader. At NMMI, if I issued a command that was not followed, I could sentence the offender to some pushups or some weekend marching in the hot sun. It was very effective.

High-involvement, high-performance, or high-commitment management practices are a much more effective approach. Empowerment is defined as giving employees the knowledge and information they need to assume more autonomy and responsibility within an organization. It is an enabling process that increases the intrinsic task motivation for employees and increases their self-efficacy—the individual's belief that he or she is capable of performing a task (Osland, et al, 2001). The outcomes of empowerment are employees who are more effective, innovative, and capable of exerting influence, and who have higher levels of job satisfaction and lower levels of stress (Spreitzer, 1995).

When I left NMMI and entered the real world of leadership as a school-age child care director, I thought that when I ordered my staff to do something, it would be done. I was shocked to find that without being able to threaten physical punishment, I had to learn some new leadership strategies. Over several years I learned that my staff needed to know why they should do a thing or learn a thing before they would do what I wanted. I learned that I had to motivate people. The point here is that I understand how empowerment can be a difficult paradigm shift for someone who is used to being the big boss. Giving power away can be a little scary, but empowering people does not mean the leader has less power; it means that the entire organization can grow to be more powerful.

## Customer Service
*Hell, there are no rules here—we're trying to accomplish something.*
*—Thomas Edison*

We travel a lot for staff training, and we often experience great and not-so-great examples of customer service. Mike has a story about a lousy customer service provider who was not empowered, not an independent thinker, and not able to make decisions and respond to changing conditions.

We were in a hotel; we arrived late at night and put a do-not-disturb sign on the door so that we could sleep as late as possible. At 10 a.m., we heard a knock at the door. I opened the door already slightly irritated at being disturbed. At the door was Faye, the head of housekeeping. She asked, "What time will you be checking out today?" I answered, "We are not checking out today, we will be here for three more nights." She looked at her clip board and said, "My paperwork shows that you check out today." I pulled out my confirmation and showed her that I was confirmed to stay for three more nights." She made an unhappy face and left without an apology. I got back into bed.

A few minutes later, there was another knock at the door. Faye was back. She said, "I printed out a new form just now and it still says you will be checking out today."

I replied, "Your form is not accurate, and we are trying to sleep." Faye said, "I just work here, and I need to get the rooms turned over."

"But we are NOT leaving today, so you don't need to turn over THIS room."

She replied, "Then there is a communication problem between the front desk and housekeeping. You'll need to go downstairs and talk to them or I'll just keep coming back every ten minutes."

I said, "If there is a communication problem between you and the front desk, YOU should go downstairs and talk to them." To which she replied, "You'll have to talk to them yourself, they won't listen to me."

This true story is one of many examples of people who feel like they have no power to make a decision or respond to a problem. They don't have a "can do" attitude because they have no power to DO anything. Since they have no real power, they hold on to the little control they do have with all their might. They are miserable and powerless and try to make others share their misery and powerlessness.

Effective leaders must establish a helpful, service-oriented culture. Give employees the knowledge and information they need, then empower them to make independent decisions and solve problems, and you will create happier staff, happier customers, and a happier YOU.

This is an example of customer service with empowered employees. We were training at a conference at a Marriott hotel, and brought our three-year-old daughter with us. Lunch was a fancy, four-course meal that was included in the conference fee. Our three-year-old was not a registered participant, so when we entered the dining room, I was worried that someone would want to see my daughter's badge or have a problem because we hadn't paid for her.

I intended to share my lunch with my daughter and so pushed the place setting away from her seat to show that I did not intend for them to serve her lunch. All waiters were rushing around the room trying to serve lunch to about two thousand people. They were very busy, so I thought they might not notice the small intruder sitting next to me.

Then I noticed one of the waiters looking at my daughter. He picked up his radio and spoke into it. As he began walking toward us I thought, "Oh no they're coming for my daughter." I assumed he was going to cause us trouble and embarrassment.

His name tag said simply, "Fred." He said, "Excuse me sir, this luncheon was prepared with adults in mind." I was opening my mouth to explain that she would only be sharing my lunch when he continued, "Would it be okay with you if I asked the kitchen to prepare her a children's meal?"

I said, "Okay, but we didn't pay for her, can I pay you directly?" Fred responded, "Oh don't worry about that." He then asked my daughter what her name was and what types of food she liked and chatted with her a bit. He noticed that she was wearing a "Birthday Girl" pin and asked if it was her birthday. She told him that she was turning four in a few days.

After preparing and serving her a special kid's meal of chicken nuggets, green beans, and french fries, the man came back with an entire chocolate cake with four candles, decorated with her name! He and several of the other extremely busy waiters then sang "Happy Birthday" to my beaming child.

The first story was about Faye, the head of housekeeping who was so NOT empowered that she couldn't even speak to the front desk. This is a story on the opposite side of the empowerment spectrum. Fred was not the "head" of anything, but a lowly waiter who was empowered to provide great customer service, to overlook the rules, and to get the kitchen staff to do something special for a customer—something that made US feel special and made us loyal customers and raving fans of the Marriott brand.

## Nuts: Customer-Friendly Skies
We fly frequently, doing staff training with early childhood educators, school-age care, and camping staff teams. For most places we fly, Southwest Airlines is the least expensive option, so we eat a lot of their nuts.

We like Southwest because the people who work there seem happy and relaxed and that makes us happy and relaxed. The employees are playful, which makes flying enjoyable. On one flight we were greeted by a flight attendant who had stuffed himself INSIDE the overhead baggage compartment. On other airlines the flight announcements are exactly the same every time, but on Southwest they might be sung to the passengers or laced with jokes. "If oxygen masks drop from the ceiling, quit screaming, let go of the person next to you….If you are traveling with children put your own mask on first and then pick the child you like the most or the one with the most potential and put that child's mask on next." On a flight with some newlyweds the flight attendants asked us all to write advice on napkins for the couple.

We noticed something unique about the culture of Southwest and recognized that it closely resembles the culture we envision in our own organization. We decided to learn more, so we did some research on Southwest's leadership (founder and former CEO Herb Kelleher) to try to determine leadership reasons for the culture. I found it! I got a chance to fly while writing this and was in a hotel shuttle van with a flight crew from Southwest. They were talking excitedly. I kept hearing the name Herb and recognized it from my research. So I eavesdropped thinking, "These people couldn't be talking about their own CEO. People at their level wouldn't even have met him." I had to ask. They WERE talking about him. They told me how much they liked him, that they had met him several times, and that he talked to them and listened to them.

Here is a brief summary of what we found. We recognize that running an airline is not exactly like leading a child care organization, but we believe many of the following leadership philosophies and beliefs are directly applicable to the leadership of ANY organization including small non-profits in the youth-serving professions.

At Southwest Airlines, the company maxim is "Hire people with a sense of humor." During interviews, applicants are asked how humor helped them out of difficult situations. Southwest Airlines does not dictate how people can or should behave when they're on the job. If they want to tell jokes, they can tell jokes (Kelleher, 1997b).

Herb Kelleher has been called the best CEO in America by Fortune magazine. Under his leadership, Southwest Airlines has become the most consistently profitable, productive, and cost-efficient carrier in the industry (Kelleher, 1997a). Kelleher credits Southwest Airlines' employees (not himself) for his company's success. He states he simply hires the best people, treats them with respect, and gives them the freedom to make decisions and to have fun being themselves (Public Broadcasting System, 2002).

Kelleher is well known for constantly flying on Southwest Airlines' planes, talking to customers and employees. This strategy comes from a customer-focused belief: "We tell our people, 'Don't worry about profit. Think about customer service.' Profit is a by-product of customer service. It's not an end in and of itself" (McConnell, 2001).

Southwest Airlines is often number one on Fortune's list of best American companies to work for (McConnell, 2001). The good-natured feelings at Southwest Airlines have everything to do with Herb Kelleher. His down-to-earth, "everyman" demeanor has endeared him to the airline's employees. His wacky behavior has helped set the tone for the airline's offbeat culture. His affinity for laughter and fun is part of Southwest Airline's culture.

Another thing that Southwest Airlines has done, culturally speaking, is that they are not just interested in people as employees. Southwest Airlines tries to honor, commemorate, celebrate, and sympathize with the things that happen to them in their personal lives (Rose, 2002). The freedom, informality, and interplay that Southwest Airlines' employees enjoy allow them to act in the best interests of the company. Kelleher once told the story of how a Southwest Airlines vice president complained several years ago that customers, gate agents, pilots, and baggage handlers had more access to Kelleher than the vice president did. Kelleher's response was, "Let me explain this: they're more important than you are" (McConnell, 2001).

Southwest has a culture of empowerment. Kelleher wrote, "A financial analyst once asked me if I was afraid of losing control of our organization. I told him I've never had control and I never wanted it. If you create an environment where the people truly participate, you don't need control" (Kelleher, 1997a). Kelleher does not look for blind obedience, but for people who on their own initiative want to be doing what they're doing because they consider it to be a worthy objective—giving people who would otherwise not be able to travel the opportunity to do so cheaply. "I have always believed that the best leader is the best server. And if you're a servant, by definition you're not controlling" (Kelleher, 1997a).

Chelsea is not a commercial airline pilot, but she has taken flying lessons and had the experience of piloting an aircraft. Imagine a pilot who sits in a cockpit surrounded by a myriad of complicated switches and gauges. She goes through her preflight checklist, step by methodical step. She submits a flight plan to air traffic control. Cleared for departure, she follows precise instructions, e.g., which runway to use, which direction to take off, what elevation to use. She communicates with flight control centers and stays within tight boundaries. She operates within a very strict system and does not have freedom to go outside that system. She doesn't think, "Hey I read this leadership book that says how important empowerment is. I have the freedom to experiment, to be creative! I think I'll mix it up a bit." Still, the crucial decisions—whether to land in high winds, whether to fly into a storm, whether to abort—rest entirely with her. She has the ultimate responsibility for the lives on the plane with her (Collins, 2001).

The point here is that empowerment to make decisions and solve problems can and should happen within boundaries. We can set strict quality standards and still empower staff to meet those standards in innovative and creative ways. Our systems are not as strict as air traffic control, since if our systems fail people don't die in a burning mass of steel. Empower your staff within the boundaries that you establish in your organization. Our leadership theory is not a warm-fuzzy philosophy reserved only for the human service, not-for-profit, or child care sectors. Empowerment is not something that is only realistic in small organizations. These theories have been proven successful even for huge and highly profitable businesses.

## Information Sharing

*The ultimate leader is one who is willing to develop people to the point that they eventually surpass him or her in knowledge and ability.*
*—Fred A. Manske, Jr.*

Sharing of information is an essential component of high-performance organizations. Ken Blanchard, world-recognized guru of leadership and customer service says, "The first key of empowerment is to share information with everyone!" It lets people understand the current situation in clear terms. It begins to build trust throughout the organization. It breaks down traditional hierarchical thinking. It helps people be more responsible, and it encourages people to act like owners of the organization.

Sharing information about financial performance, administrative strategies, and long-term planning sends a message that the organization's people are trusted. Chelsea teaches a college course on child care management. This is her story. When it is time to teach about budget development, I ask my students to bring in a copy of the budget from their own organization. I was at first surprised and continue to be disheartened at how many students are not allowed to see the budget of the organization they work for. They tell me that their directors tell them that the information is confidential and can only be seen by the owner and center director. If you want to create a high-involvement organization, you can't have secrets.

Employees of empowering organizations know not only what is happening in the organization but why and how it could affect their jobs and careers. If you want staff at all levels to show good fiscal management skills, to conserve supplies, to feel ownership and responsibility for the financial strength of your organization, they NEED to share in the information. "Open-book" management creates ownership and shared responsibility. People without information cannot act responsibly. People with information are compelled to act responsibly. Sharing information motivates employees by providing relevancy. Employees must have all of the knowledge and information they need to effectively exercise the power and control they must have to be self-directed. Give your organization's budget information or your program budget to your staff. Teach them how to read and analyze it. Spend time discussing it and answering questions.

## Training and Professional Development
Training is often seen as a frill in many organizations—something to be cut if

profits diminish. This is an example of the short-term thinking that enslaves managers and inhibits the development of a high-involvement organization. Knowledge and skill are crucial to organizations, and too few organizations designate their resources in ways that honor this insight. Training involves establishing clear boundaries and high expectations that build upon information sharing. Ken Blanchard's second key to empowerment is to "Create autonomy through boundaries." Boundaries establish a purpose; they define the "business of the business." They establish values and operational guidelines. They establish long-term strategic thinking. They help translate the goals for the organization and roles for the stakeholders. The vision of an organization truly becomes alive when everyone sees where his or her contribution can make a difference. Training is a vehicle to these ends.

When typical organizations do spend money and time on training, most training covers policies and procedures. It often includes how to handle situations according to "upper management." Instead of teaching staff members only "how" to do something, teach them "why." Teach staff members how to problem solve. How to identify a problem and how to think about all the options they have available to them. When you spend training time and energy on explaining the standard or the "boundary" and how to solve problems you empower your staff. Let the team decide how to best meet the expectation with their available resources. Every team and every site has different situations. The traditional mold won't work for everyone.

Training leads to empowerment by teaching others things they can do to become less dependent on you. Training is an essential component of high-involvement organizations because this paradigm relies on "frontline" employee skill and initiative to identify, solve problems, initiate solutions, serve the needs of families, and take responsibility for safety and quality.

You will know when you are giving your staff enough information because they will need you less. It may begin to feel like you are no longer a good leader. Before founding our organization, Chelsea was the director of a large corporate child care center in New Mexico. This is her story. The company had over a hundred centers across the nation, and we often got together for retreats and training events. At every break at one of my first retreats all the directors in my division would rush into the hall to return pages or phone messages with their staff back at their centers. I never got one message. I began to feel useless and not needed. I made this comment to my regional manager and she told me something very memorable. She said, "Chelsea, it is a sign of a good leader when your staff do not need you. You have trained them well."

## Decentralized Power and Control
*He who has never learned to obey cannot be a good commander.*
*—Aristotle*

Ken Blanchard's third key to empowerment is "To replace hierarchy with self-directed work teams!" Less bureaucratic, elitist, hierarchical, and authoritarian organizations can create self-managed teams that are more communicative, participatory, and empowered. Self-managed teams permit removal of layers of hierarchy and absorption of administrative tasks. Empowered TEAMS can do more than empowered INDIVIDUALS. Teams with information and training can replace hierarchy. When power and control are decentralized all of the people in the organization feel accountable and responsible for the success of the organization and the accomplishment of the mission. Child care and youth development organizations are a uniquely good fit for self-managed teams because individual sites provide a cellular structure for the identification of these teams. Each site can become a self-managed team, trained and empowered to facilitate the positive development of children and meet the needs of families.

In a classic experiment, management gave factory employees a lever that controlled how fast they could operate the assembly line. They were at first afraid that employees would take advantage and slow down production. They were later surprised that employees actually worked faster when they felt in control of their work. Employees who participate in decision making, collecting information, generating alternatives, and implementing decisions have an increased sense of control and commitment. In our organization, all staff members participate in developing policy, designing their own evaluation instruments, and making all hiring decisions. Caregivers participate in the hiring decisions of their potential site directors and thereby become more committed to the supervisor who is eventually hired. (See chapter 9 for more information about this group interviewing process.) Self-directed teams lead to increased job satisfaction; an attitude change from "have to" to "want to;" greater employee commitment; better communication between employees and management; a more efficient decision-making process; improved quality of services; reduced operating expenses; and a more profitable and successful organization.

As mentioned before, Chelsea teaches a college course on child care management. This is her story. Every semester I have my students ask a panel of my site directors leadership questions. One of my students asked the panel if any of them had ever thought of owning their own child care program. The unanimous answer from the directors sums up the purpose of sharing as much knowledge, information, power and control perfectly. The answer all my directors gave was they don't need to own their own program because they already feel that they own this program. That is the benefit of giving power and control to well-trained staff—a sense of ownership!

## Delegation

*The surest way for an executive to kill himself is to refuse to learn how, and when, and to whom to delegate work.*
—J. C. Penney

The old maxim is, "Don't just stand there, do something!" To empower people, sometimes you have to know how to follow the new rule, "Don't just do something—stand there!" High-involvement organizations require trust and the willingness to let employees do what they know how to do. After giving employees the knowledge and information needed to exercise control, leaders must give them the opportunity to make decisions. This means that leaders must sometimes allow them to make mistakes and to learn from their mistakes.

When leaders do not delegate they neglect their responsibility of nurturing the leadership skills of others. I suggest that the primary responsibility of a site director is to mentor and train and develop new directors from a team of caregivers. Delegation is essential to developing new leadership and directors from within. Ralph Nader says, "I start with the premise that the function of leadership is to produce more leaders, not more followers."

Mike's father, who operated under the "old school" paradigm often said, "If you want something done right, you'd better do it yourself." This philosophy is wise under certain conditions, such as a very personal task done for personal reasons, something that is already a strength of yours. For example, if I am a great wood worker and I want a new rocking chair, customized to my body and preferences; it might be in my own best interest to make it myself. In other situations it is better to hire an expert, such as hiring an electrician to upgrade the wiring in your house. As an organizational leader, if you are a "control freak," insisting on doing many tasks yourself because you believe you can do the things you do better than anyone else, you might be imposing limits on your own growth and the growth of your followers. If you insist on doing it all yourself, you are inhibiting the culture of a high-involvement organization.

This is easier to do when relating it to children. As educators, we know that children learn best by doing. Children can't learn to tie their shoes if we always tie the laces for them and never expect them to do it. Children can't learn to share toys when we swoop in and take them away at the first hint of an argument. This concept is also more tangible when relating it to coaches. Coaches don't call a time-out, run over to the mound, and take over for the pitcher who is doing poorly. This seems absurd. The same is true for leading. Doing all the work yourself should seem absurd.

Some managers tend to believe that the greater degree of their own supervision and involvement, the better the work produced. They also genuinely believe that they are more capable than others. They believe that work done under more oversight and control will be better than identical work performed with less oversight. Again, this is short-term thinking. By delegating, not menial and mindless tasks, but important, challenging tasks to constituents, they grow stronger and more competent in the long-term. Delegating isn't giving people empowerment and then washing your hands of the matter. Empowerment means people have the freedom to act; but it also means they must be held accountable for their results.

The point here is to delegate authority, but stay involved. Check in on their progress to see what resources you may be able to offer. Acknowledge their efforts and successes.

## Try This: Empowerment Exercise

A true leader needs to share knowledge, information, power, and control. Make a list of when you have shared power and control with your subordinates in the last six months. If the list is long, you are on the right track. If it is a pretty short list, make a list of things you could have shared but did not. Now work on sharing those things in the future.

## Reduction of Status Differences

High-involvement organizations must attempt to reduce the status distinctions that separate individuals and groups and cause some to feel less valued. This can be accomplished through the intentional use of language, labels, and physical space, as well as the degree of wage disparity across levels. In the past, our organization gave all employees staff shirts. The directors received shirts with collars and the caregivers received t-shirts. This was a purely financial decision (collared shirts cost more, and we have fewer directors), but it sent a message that the directors were professionals and the caregivers were not. We have since given all staff collared shirts. It costs more, but we eliminated this distinction which we didn't want to convey.

Directors can reduce status differences by not designating work roles according to hierarchical distinctions. When directors assume a share of housekeeping duties at a site, when upper-level administrators work "in the ratios" with the children when needed, when caregivers lead large group discussion groups or lead the staff meetings, status differences are minimized and staff are empowered.

## Servant Leadership

*The first responsibility of a leader is to define reality. The last is to say thank you. In between, the leader is a servant.*
—*Max DePree*

Robert Greenleaf researched management, leadership, and education for forty years. He felt that the power-centered authoritarian leadership style so prominent in U.S. institutions was not working, and in 1964 he took an early retirement to found the Center for Applied Ethics. He was captivated by the idea of a servant actually being the leader. He wrote, "I came to believe that we in this country were in a leadership crisis and that I should do what I could about it." In 1970, he published his first essay, entitled The Servant as Leader, which introduced the term "servant leadership." Later, the essay was expanded into a book, which is perhaps one of the most influential management texts ever written.

The Servant Leadership movement was born. Greenleaf believed that service to followers is the primary responsibility of leaders (Yukl, 2002). In traditional top-down hierarchical organizations, the managers at the top of the pyramid seize and hold back knowledge, information, power, and control. In our organization, leaders teach their constituents and give them opportunities to develop their skills. They "serve" their followers, giving them the knowledge, information, and resources they need do their jobs and to develop. Servant leaders are givers not takers. They give power away in order to develop leadership skills in their followers.

The servant leader must empower followers instead of using power to dominate them. Servant leaders choose to give power away for a purpose larger than themselves. They take the power that flows into them and transfer it to others.

Servant leaders are both learners and teachers. They use power in the service and development of others and are driven by values. In our organization, I often say to colleagues who, according to a formal hierarchical organizational chart, are our subordinates, "You don't work for me, I work for you." Servant leaders are learners. They listen to followers about their needs and aspirations. Their door is always open. They are out talking and listening to people at all levels of the organization (Pollard, 1996). Leaders must listen, take advice, lose arguments, and follow (Kouzes & Posner, 1995). They must be willing to walk a mile in the other person's shoes.

Servant leaders are teachers. They help their followers to become healthier, wiser, and more competent in meeting their responsibilities. A servant leader increases another's sense of self-confidence, self-determination, and personal effectiveness and makes that person more powerful, greatly enhancing the possibility of success (Kouzes & Posner, 1995). They nurture, protect and empower their followers. Leaders develop their constituents and serve them by providing meaningful and rewarding work.

Servant leaders are values driven. Trust is established by being completely honest and open with their followers, keeping their actions consistent with their values and showing trust in followers (Pollard, 1996). Servant leaders ask their followers what they can do to help them do their jobs better. They ask them what resources they need. Resources may be supplies, more staff, or more knowledge. The job of a servant leader is not to tell followers how to do a better job, but to get the resources they need or have requested to be more successful. The servant leader must look out for the best interests of the followers, standing up for what is right, even if it is not in the best financial interest of the organization (Yukl, 2002). A leader who is willing to serve can provide hope instead of gloom and can be an example for those who want direction and purpose in their lives and who desire to accomplish and contribute.

## Caring About People

*You do not lead by hitting people over the head—that's assault; not leadership.*
*—Dwight D. Eisenhower*

One mental model about good leadership is enormously perverse in its implication: good managers are mean or tough. The ability to make such tough decisions as laying off people and acting decisively are considered by many to be signs of strong leadership. Good leaders view their constituents as volunteers, not in that they work for free, but knowing that they have choices about where they work. Employees who don't feel recognized or appreciated—who feel that no matter how much they do, it is never enough—who don't have fun at work—are living examples of employee burnout. High-involvement organizations demand committed employees who freely give their emotional, intellectual, and physical energy to the success of the organization and the accomplishment of the mission. These employees are created by leaders who care about them as people and provide them with all the knowledge, information, power, and control we've been discussing in this chapter.

## Challenging Work and Shared Values

Employees who feel personally committed to shared goals and values are more likely to work hard to accomplish them. Employee commitment often comes from a leader who shares their values and a mission that passionately communicates why their work is important. Boring work is drudgery; it is physically and mentally draining; and lots of boring work is deadly to an organization. Asking employees to do increasing amounts of boring work is self-defeating. The culture of an organization is crucial to creating high-involvement organizations. A culture of common values and challenging work is fun and rewarding—part of the compensation for working in this type of organization. Establishing, striving for, and accomplishing the mission should be energizing, exciting, fun, and worthy of celebration.

## Try This: Take the Time

Take the time to get to know personal things about your staff and help them get to know each other. Be interested in their lives. Remember and celebrate their birthdays. Take the time for "small talk." Hold family social events and show honor and respect for their families. What are their hopes, dreams, and aspirations?

## Try This: Kids' Council

Empowerment starts with the kids. Form a Kids' Council. The kids are empowered to solve problems and make decisions. When it is time to purchase new games, the Kids' Council surveys the "little kids" to find out what games they want. We take them to the store to pick out the games. They develop a sense of ownership over the games, so they take good care of them. When there is a problem to solve, we often give it to the Kids' Council. They identify the problem, create a goal, brainstorm for solutions, pick a strategy, implement the strategy, and evaluate the outcome.

## Bringing It Home

*The best executive is the one who has sense enough to pick good men to do what he wants them to do, and self-restraint enough to keep from meddling while they do it.*
*—Teddy Roosevelt*

Empowerment is an important foundation in school-age care and youth development and must be shared by children and staff members. "Individuals who have choice are empowered, and empowerment increases the likelihood of commitment" (Schlechty, 1997, p. 155). Empowerment in caregivers leads to commitment to the shared goals and philosophies, which leads to better care, which leads to better student behavior, which leads to increased caregiver commitment, and so on (an amplifying feedback loop with exponentially growing desirable effects). Caregivers need to have considerable influence and control over decisions about their time and the way it is used, their physical space and how it is utilized, and the way knowledge and information should be organized into a curriculum that is presented to children, if they are to be empowered (Schlechty, 1997).

Our organization empowers caregivers, blurring the line between the administration and the caregivers. The caregivers AND administrators are involved with the children and families daily, and they all participate in making decisions about agency policy and practices. They are given the professional development opportunities and the time needed for this level of involvement. We do not abruptly relocate control to the lowest levels of the organization and simply wash our hands of all leadership at the upper levels.

Control is portioned out according to knowledge and responsibility. It is a continuous, dynamic process. Caregivers must be helped to acquire the knowledge they need to facilitate positive development more powerfully, as well as make decisions about running their programs and allocation of resources. In some organizations, one person writes the curriculum for staff. In our organization, caregivers begin planning activities under the coaching supervision of more experienced caregivers, which eventually leads to them writing their own curriculum for enrichment clubs.

In some organizations, a human resources department hires new employees and assigns them to a program. In our organization, entry-level caregivers are paid to participate in interviewing prospective staff members. When the interview is over, we ask them their opinion first. Then we process everyone's opinions as a team. This experience helps them learn what traits we are looking for in themselves and in others. Eventually, they learn to make sound hiring decisions.

In many organizations a supervisor evaluates his subordinates. In our organization, when it is time for an evaluation, caregivers evaluate themselves and then their peers evaluate them. After that their supervisors meet with them to process all of the feedback together. Through this experience, they learn what performance standards are expected, and what those standards look like in themselves and others.

In the learning community of our organization, the learning that occurs in staff meetings, at staff training events, and during everyday conversation between caregivers is about the great subject of child learning and child development (Palmer, 1998). Systems thinking teaches us that systems are in a constant state of change, so caregivers will constantly and necessarily need to change their perspectives and knowledge about teaching and learning, critically reflecting on their practices in light of new knowledge.

In this empowering organization, the caregiver is a valued, empowered, trusted professional with expertise that is utilized to its fullest potential. The caregiver is supported and further empowered by administration that is trained on and committed to collaboratively developing practices, which are best for the development and education of children and families. When the caregivers are empowered as leaders of the organization, and broaden their approaches and take responsibility for all aspects of the learning community, the vision of this future-focused, empowering, high-involvement organization can become a reality.

## Conclusion

Employees with no power are lousy to work with. They say things like, "I JUST work here." That is how they feel and that is how they act. They do the minimum required of them to get their paycheck. When people are empowered they feel like they own the place, like they have a stake in the reputation of the organization. Empowerment creates a sense of ownership and relevancy in everyone in the organization: kids, caregivers, assistants, and directors.

## Discussion Questions

1. Do you have horror stories about terrible service you have received? Do you have examples of great service? Think about the people responsible for the service you received. Were they empowered or not?

2. Think about your current job. What power does your boss withhold from you? What would you like more power and control over?

3. What power do you withhold from your staff? What can you delegate to your staff to help them grown and learn and develop?

4. Does your boss share all the information with you that you need to do your job well? Do you withhold information from your staff? Do they have the information they need about the budget or about how the organization operates that would help them to feel more ownership?

5. Can you identify status differences in your organization? Do people in power get special perks that the more "lowly" people are denied? Are these differences necessary?

## Helpful Resources

*Empowerment Takes More Than a Minute by Ken Blanchard* (Author), Publisher: Berrett-Koehler Publishers; 2nd ed. edition (October 10, 2001). ISBN-10: 1576751538

For more from Ken Blanchard, visit
www.kenblanchard.com

## Reference Notes

Chief Executive (1999). Chief executive of the year. Retrieved September 29, 2003, from http://www.chiefexecutive.net/mag/146/article1.htm

Greenleaf, R.K. (2003). *The servant-leader within: a transformative path*. New York: Paulist Press.

Greenleaf, R. K. (2002). *Servant leadership: A journey into the nature of legitimate power and greatness* (25th anniversary ed.). New York: Paulist Press.

Kelleher, H. (1997b). Testimony before the National Civil Aviation Review Commission. Retrieved September 27, 2003, from http://www.library.unt.edu/gpo/NCARC/testimony/swa-te.htm

Kelleher, H. (1997a). A Culture of Commitment. *Leader to Leader*. 4 (Spring 1997): 20–24.

McConnell, B. (2001). The wild flying turkey with wings. Retrieved September 15, 2002, from http://www.creatingcustomerevangelists.com/resources/evangelists/herb_kelleher.asp

Public Broadcasting System (2002). Innovators: Herb Kelleher. Retrieved September 29, 2003, from http://www.pbs.org/kcet/chasingthesun/innovators/hkelleher.html

Rose, C. (2002). Q&A with Southwest's Herb Kelleher. Retrieved September 29, 2003, from http://business.cisco.com/prod/tree.taf

Southwest Airlines (2002). Time flies when you're having fun. Retrieved September 10, 2002, from http://www.iflyswa.com/about_swa/airborne.html

# Part IV: The Details

# Chapter 7: Influencing the Individuals

*Pull the string, and it will follow wherever you wish. Push it, and it will go nowhere at all.*
—*Dwight D. Eisenhower*

*Leadership is getting someone to do what they don't want to do, to achieve what they want to achieve.*
—*Tom Landry*

*People are Strange.*
—*The Doors*

### Introduction
*The key to successful leadership today is influence, not authority.*
—*Ken Blanchard*

Leadership is about influence, not power. Great leaders know how to tap into the hearts and minds of their followers. If you stand and look over the shoulders of those you supervise, you'll never get people who care about their jobs. The key to successful leadership is learning how to motivate staff. This chapter does not preach the old "carrot and stick" approach to motivation. Rather, it will teach you how to get intrinsic, true, inner motivation

According to the old-school organizational cliché, what gets rewarded gets done. So, many organizations offer rewards such as profit-sharing, bonuses, awards, prizes, and special parking spaces to motivate employees. These are classic examples of extrinsic rewards, or token/tangible rewards given to employees. Our philosophy is that what is rewarding gets done. "We can never pay people enough to care—to care about their products, services, communities, or families, or even the bottom line. True leaders tap into peoples' hearts and minds, not merely their hands and wallets" (Kouzes & Posner, 1995, p. 40). These are intrinsic rewards, rewards that come from within the person.

"Accentuating the intrinsic rewards of tasks rather than emphasizing an external rationale creates higher levels of commitment. Employees who work hard primarily for the big bucks are unlikely to be able to sustain energy and effort over the long haul" (Kouzes & Posner, 1995, p. 254). Human organizations, be they homeless shelters, schools, or child care programs, can give employees the opportunity to make a difference to society, to facilitate the positive development of children, to prevent juvenile delinquency, to develop productive citizens, and in the long term to make healthier families and healthier communities possible.

"Pay and other external rewards can significantly lower intrinsic motivation and can create dependence upon expensive reward systems" (Kouzes & Posner, 1995, p. 41). In situations that are already intrinsically rewarding, the addition of extrinsic rewards may reduce the effectiveness of the intrinsic rewards (Deci, 1975; Kouzes & Posner, 1995; Kohn, 1999). Extrinsic rewards are effective in teaching a rat to run a maze, but are not effective in teaching an adult to demonstrate ideal performance. Brain research shows us that while external rewards may temporarily increase desired physical responses, they actually decrease desired complex behaviors (Jensen, 1998).

Short-term behavior changes sometimes result from external rewards, but for those changes to last, it is necessary to keep the rewards coming. Employers often utilize token reward programs, such as employee of the month awards associated with a gift certificate, to promote desirable behavior. An examination of the research shows this to be invalid. Further, rewards actually lessen the engagement a human feels about the learning activity. Staff members who are not rewarded for desirable behavior actually feel more commitment to the behavior than staff members who are rewarded for desirable behavior (Kohn, 1999).

Rewards fail to make deep lasting changes because they are aimed at affecting only what people do and not at what they think and feel. If employers want to do nothing more than induce compliance in employees, then rewards may be a valid practice. If employers want staff members to be self-disciplined, self-motivated workers, then rewards are worse than useless; they are counterproductive (Kohn, 1999).

## Learning is Motivation

People have an intrinsic desire to learn. Praise and manipulation can only serve to stifle that natural motivation and replace it with blind conformity, a mechanical work style, or open defiance toward authority (Hitz & Driscoll, 1988). In a study of about a hundred mothers in California, researchers studied the mothers and children from the time the children were one year old until they were eight years old. They looked into those who pushed their kids to do well in school, especially those who rewarded good grades or removed privileges for bad grades. The children of these mothers became less interested in learning and were less likely to succeed in school. The more that school achievement was the main concern of the parent, the lower was the commitment of the children (Kohn, 1999). These observations about basic principles of human motivation apply to adults as well as children, both of whom are driven by intrinsic motivation.

Intrinsic motivation must be present if people are to do their best. "If work comes to be seen solely as a source of money and never as a source of fulfillment, organizations will totally ignore other human needs at work—needs involving such intangibles as learning, self-worth, pride, competence, and serving others" (Kouzes & Posner, 1995, p. 41). Motivation must be internalized; internal rewards maximize intrinsic motivation.

## Pleasure is Motivation

What makes something intrinsically motivating; a reward in itself? People find things intrinsically motivating if they derive pleasure from the experience and pleasure from using their skills, and if they feel that their work is challenging and adventurous (Csikszentmihaly, 1975; Kouzes & Posner, 1995). "Being invited to do better than we've ever done before compels us to reach deep down inside and bring forth the adventurer within" (Kouzes & Posner, 1995, p. 42). Intrinsic rewards include a sense of accomplishment, born in the thrill of creation; rewards that are the outcome of individual effort. Giving the director of a child care and youth development program the opportunities to create new programs and develop new strategies for helping people is a reward linked to performance. Although intrinsic motivation comes from inside the individual, it is not something outside of the influence and control of organizational leaders. For leaders to get the best from others, they must "Find opportunities for people to

solve problems, make discoveries, explore new ground, reach difficult goals, or…
make work responsibilities fun" (Kouzes & Posner, 1995, p. 42).

## Try This: Double Your Pleasure

Make a list of the pleasurable experiences people have at your organization. What is fun? Now ask other employees to create a list. How do your lists compare? Think of ways to add more pleasure and fun.

## Acknowledgement is Motivation

When leaders lend a hand with the work being done, when they actively listen to employees without interrupting, and when they give sincere verbal recognition in public, they take an active role in increasing the intrinsic rewards of good performance. Motivating leaders can provide feedback and coaching at the time of employee performance to enhance intrinsic motivation. Showing genuine concern and respect for those doing the work boosts intrinsic motivation.

Imagine you are in your work setting and your supervisor approaches you and says, "Excuse me, do you have a moment? I'd like to talk to you." What would be your first thoughts? Yep, what did I do now, what am in trouble for? When supervisors only provide positive feedback and acknowledgement during a staff meeting or at an annual evaluation, when it is "planned" acknowledgement, it seems fake. Good leaders carefully observe their followers and seek out opportunities to provide on-the-spot feedback. Spontaneous and unexpected acknowledgement and appreciation for good work and for effort in and of itself is effective for developing intrinsic motivation. In fact, personal congratulations rank at the top of the most powerful non-financial motivators identified by employees (Kouzes & Posner, 1995).

Congratulations and social recognition from other team members are often the most valued rewards for teambuilding behaviors. Recognition from team members is particularly likely to occur when the team is held accountable for team performance and any recognition from management goes to the team and not to individual team members. When management recognizes individual team members, other members are not as motivated to provide recognition themselves because they grow to see this as the responsibility of management. Team members tend to want recognition from their peers more than they want it from management. Teamwork rightly places individual achievement within the context of organizational and team goals.

## Try This: Acknowledge Effort

Think about how often people are appreciated in your organization. Find at least three more ways employees can be acknowledged for their work. Make sure to acknowledge effort as well as success and help create a climate where everyone, not just the leader, acknowledges each other.

## Meaning is Motivation

One reason internalization is so important is that it links prior and new learning together, which creates meaning and the intrinsic motivation for good performance and continued learning. "There are sweeping sociocultural changes as employees are seeking a deeper sense of meaning from their worklives" (Rolls, 1995, p. 102). People are intrinsically motivated to be involved in work that is aligned with their own values and interests, with work that is worthwhile and has relevancy or meaning for them as individuals. As people seek heightened authenticity, compassion, wholeness, and meaning outside of work, their newfound growth and expectations will come to work with them. Articulating the inherent goodness of the work being done by the director of the school-age care program and the benefit it has to society is an important factor.

Leaders create meaning by helping employees to see and foresee cause and effect by pointing out the connections between their actions and consequences. Leaders create meaning by engaging the emotions of employees. Leaders create meaning through a caring environment, by eliminating stress and threat, meeting basic physical needs, ensuring safety, and establishing boundaries and expectations. Leaders create meaning through positive relationships by providing adult role models, caring authoritative relationships, positive peer relationships, and positive interactive feedback. Leaders create meaning through positive experiences which are purposefully planned to provide novelty, playfulness, challenge, enrichment, community building, and problem solving.

The easiest way to accomplish this is through building relationships with your followers. I'm not saying you have to be friends with everyone, or for that matter even LIKE them. However, understanding systems thinking helps us realize that the more you truly care about your staff, the more they will care about their job and their work will improve. So, if you do not like someone, work hard at finding some things you do like about that person (find the pony). Find ways to let go of work responsibilities and learn to care deeply for all your team members.

"Employees want to enjoy work, to feel they can make a contribution, to feel respected as people and to learn and grow" (Rolls, 1995, p. 102). Psychologist David E. Berlew believes that what really excites people and generates enthusiasm are these value-related opportunities—a chance to be tested, to make it on one's own, to take part in a social experiment, to do something well, to do something good, and to change the way things are (Kouzes & Posner, 1995). Followers want to be a part of something significant, and for their work to have real meaning and relevancy. Effective leaders understand the desires of followers and work to make their work relevant. "Without employing people's hearts, organizations lose precious return on their investment in people" (Kouzes & Posner, 1995, p. 41).

People need the opportunity to do something deeply moral, meaningful and transforming in their work life. Leaders can create meaning for work and learning by helping employees to see and foresee cause and effect, by pointing out the connections between their actions and consequences, and by showing the logical reasons for their tasks. It is important for organizational leaders to recognize that in order for people to learn something so that it is easy for them to use it, it must be logical, moral, and fun (Kline & Saunders, 1998).

### Relevancy is Motivation

Imagine that we put up a painting, and around it is an old beat-up scratched frame. Does the frame influence your perception of the picture? We suspect so. Now imagine, instead of that old frame we put up a brand new, beautiful frame lighted just right. Does that influence your perception? Again, we suspect so, although the painting never changed. Frames are how we choose to look at something. We learn from our experiences, yes, but what we learn depends upon the frame we put around it. Frames establish relevancy. They answer the question of "what's in it for me?" WIIFM?

Framing is a great tool for motivating people. If I command someone to do something, I might get obedience, but not motivation because there is no relevancy. If we want our staff to attend a training event, we might say, "I know that your weekends are precious to you, but licensing requires that you all get twenty-four clock hours of training per year. This Saturday there is a training event and it is mandatory, so don't be late, and don't forget to get a signature on your certificate to prove that you were there." Wow, wouldn't you be excited to be at that training? No? What if we framed it like this? "I have noticed that the children in your program sometimes misbehave and this stresses you out. I've got good news for you. We've found someone who conducts a great training on guidance. In just one day you can learn some skills that will reduce your stress, make your job easier, and get the kinds of behavior that makes you truly LOVE working with these kids!" Better right? It is still the same training event, but with a different frame.

Framing can work with employees, bosses, even spouses. If you can't positively frame something you want your staff to do or learn, reconsider whether you need them to do it. If it is important to do, then find a frame that fits! Think about the person and what is relevant to them, not how it is relevant to YOU.

Our older daughter was a little afraid of the water. We planned to take a vacation one summer to spend some time with friends who happen to have a lake house: jet skis, motorboat, a dock to jump off of into the lake. We thought it was important for her to learn how to swim. When she'd try to put her head under water, typically only part of her face would get wet. We enrolled her in swimming lessons. She was in the pool with a group of six-year olds. Her swimming teacher was a young man.

He began the class by saying, "Okay kids, it is really important for you to learn what I'm going to teach you in this class." I grinned really big and looked at Chelsea and said, "Cool—he's about to FRAME it!" Chelsea said, "You are such a dork!"

The swimming teacher continued, "The reason it is so important for you to learn what I'm going to teach you is that at the end of this class there will be a test. If you don't learn this then you can't pass into the more advanced class next summer." I shook my head in disgust. He missed a great opportunity to establish relevancy.

When we got home, Chelsea and I put a new frame around the lessons. "Madison, we're going to the lake house this summer. Last summer when we went there you had to wear the life jacket all the time. It was big and bulky. You couldn't go on the boat or the jet skis or do a lot of the things you wanted to do because you couldn't swim. You were afraid of the water. We were thinking that if you learned to swim really well, you wouldn't be afraid, you wouldn't have to wear the life jacket all the time, and you'd have more fun in the water! How does that sound to you?" That summer the little girl who would only dunk part of her face under water was jumping off the dock, laughing and squealing and having fun with the other kids.

## Team Spirit is Motivation

*The secret is to work less as individuals and more as a team. As a coach, I play not my eleven best, but my best eleven.*
—*Knute Rockne*

*The way a team plays as a whole determines its success. You may have the greatest bunch of individual stars in the world, but if they don't play together, the club won't be worth a dime.*
—*Babe Ruth*

Learning the content of teamwork and followership in a practical, real-world context is important for relevancy and motivation. In order for work teams to be successful and stay together, there must be a clear and interesting goal. This goal must be exciting, chosen by the team, and agreed upon by all members.

The team must possess the social capital to be successful: cooperation, collaboration, and mutual assistance. The most important element in building this social capital is trust; all else flows from it. Informal, seeming irrelevant, day-to-day conversations among employees build trust that will make their working relationships more effective in the future (Lipnack & Stamps, 2001).

Chelsea is the financial manager of our organization, and found this extremely hard to accept. She often finds herself in her office working at the computer while other members of the organization are in the other room. She can hear them chatting and if she just keeps her financial manager hat on all she can see are the payroll dollar signs adding up with little productivity. However, she has also seen

130

the benefit first hand of this chatting among employees. Our team members know and care deeply for each other. They trust each other and are willing to help each other out when needed. It is hard to put a price on this.

Another element is reciprocity—give and take. People need to trust that giving will eventually result in receiving. That making a sacrifice to benefit others is an investment that will yield returns in the future. Over the last few years, we have worked hard on sharing staff among sites. We have had many conversations with directors about giving up good staff for a while, even if it makes it more stressful at their site, to help other sites that are extremely short staffed. It was difficult at first as directors were not completely trusting that they would receive the same help if they needed it. After many exchanges, they learned to trust that reciprocity would happen, and our team is now closer and the organization has an easier time sharing.

## Story Time: Goose Sense

Mike's dad had an expression. He used to say, "Mike, you don't have the sense that God gave a goose!" I'm still not sure exactly what he meant by that, but I'm pretty sure I should get some therapy. Fortunately, now I know a little more about goose sense.

When you see geese heading south for the winter, flying in "V" formation, you might be interested in knowing what science has discovered about why they fly that way. It has been learned that as each bird flaps its wings, it creates uplift for the bird immediately following. By flying in a "V" formation, the whole flock adds at least 71 percent greater flying range than if each bird flew on its own.

Whenever a goose falls out of formation, it suddenly feels the drag and resistance of trying to go it alone, and quickly gets back into formation to take advantage of the lifting power of the bird immediately in front.

When the lead goose gets tired, he rotates back in the wing and another goose flies point. The geese honk from behind to encourage those up front to keep up their speed. Finally, when a goose gets sick, or is wounded by gunshot and falls out, two geese fall out of formation and follow him down to help protect him.

They stay with him until he is either able to fly or until he is dead, and then they launch out on their own or with another formation to catch up with their group. If we have the sense of a goose, we will stand by each other like that! People who share a common direction and sense of community can get where they are going quicker and easier, because they are traveling on the thrust of one another. If we have as much sense as a goose, we will stay in formation with those who are headed the same way we are going. It also pays to take turns doing hard jobs.

## Try This: Teambuilding

Take the time to focus on teambuilding. There are countless books on teambuilding initiatives. We've listed a few favorites in the Helpful Resources section in this chapter. In our organization, each summer we take our summer staff on a two-day retreat in the mountains of New Mexico to focus on teambuilding. Sometimes we do teambuilding games on the ground, and sometimes we do them on low or high ropes up in the trees. We have found them to be a lot of fun and very effective.

## Rewarding A While Hoping for B

There are many examples of reward systems that reward undesirable behaviors while ignoring desired behavior. Soldiers are rewarded with bed rest and rehabilitation when they exhibit fatigue-based disobedience. Politicians who tell people what they want to hear and make empty promises are rewarded by being elected. Professors who spend more time on research than on teaching are rewarded for publishing articles—"publish or perish." Athletes who put themselves ahead of their team are rewarded and recognized for outstanding individual performance. Children who skip school are "rewarded" with a suspension from school under the guise of "punishment." Doctors are financially rewarded when they provide treatment for patients who are not sick.

There may be many causes for "rewarding A while hoping for B." Many organizations like to use simple, black and white, quantifiable standards to assess performance, which often ignore many desirable, though more intangible behaviors. There is an overemphasis on highly visible behaviors, which results in rewarding homeruns above teamwork, and published articles above classroom teaching. People sometimes reward undesirable behavior out of a sense of morality, equity, or some "higher calling." For example, welfare benefits and social programs reward poor people who don't work.

Personnel policies on sick leave are often based on a "use it or lose it" philosophy. All employees have a certain number of paid sick leave days per year. Sick days may or may not be accumulated and saved for future use. The result is that employees who use sick days get more annual days of leave than employees who do not use as many sick days. If employees do not use sick days, then they work more days per year but are compensated the same as employees who use all of their sick days. This reward system encourages people who are completely well or mildly ill to "take" unnecessary sick days so that they avoid the feeling of being cheated.

Organizations often reward individual performance above teamwork even though they encourage and hope for a high level of teamwork among their employees. After all, teamwork is in the best interest of most organizations. Teamwork results in reduced absenteeism, lower turnover, increased employee motivation, greater growth satisfaction, social satisfaction, and trust (Osland, et al, p. 192). Nevertheless, most organizations reward employees solely for individual performance, so most employees focus solely on their own individual performance. Employees are rewarded when they show that they are the best, when they stand out, when they are "head and shoulders above the crowd."

Performance assessment tools typically focus solely on individual performance. Organizations often designate a certain amount of money for salary increases. Raises are portioned out based on individual merit, putting team members in competition for rewards. "Particularly destructive are performance-appraisal systems for individuals that require a fixed number of positive and negative ratings or provide fixed pots of budget money that need to be divided up differentially among the individuals in a group" (Lawler, 1992, p. 197). Promotions and advancement opportunities are also given to the individual who performs better than the other members of the team. Advancement is viewed as an opportunity to break the bonds of following by advancing to a position as a leader. Team-based rewards ensure that all team members get the same size bonus or salary increase. When our entire organization meets budget expectations while also providing high quality, the entire team gets a salary increase.

"Is it better to be a leader or a follower?" Ask this question and most respondents will answer that it is better to be a leader. Few children aspire to grow up and become followers. Parents and teachers instruct that following is a mindless act of stupidity, illustrated by the familiar question, "Would you jump off a cliff just because everyone else was jumping off a cliff?" Douglas Smith, author of *Taking Charge*, and coauthor of *The Wisdom of Teams*, says that "Following suffers from a serious image problem" (Smith, 1996, p. 202).

As we've stated earlier, our organization requires all staff to be leaders. However, they can't be leaders all at the same time. If the organization wants everyone to work together, but the culture of the organization is one of competition to be promoted to a higher position, then it is rewarding individual performance while hoping for teamwork. Followers are important for teamwork. Good followers are a key element in leadership. Groups in which everyone tries to lead or push his or her own agenda are dysfunctional—as the familiar saying goes, "Too many chefs in the kitchen spoil the broth" (Brethower & Smalley, 1998). Many times the decision of who should lead must be made based on the situation, not on individual job titles.

In the twenty-first century organization, effective leaders must learn to follow if they are to successfully lead. The omniscient leader is obsolete. Effective leaders must pay close attention to situations in which their most effective option is to follow—not because the hierarchy demands that they "obey," but because building a great organization requires them to rely on the capacities and insights of other people (Smith, 1996).

Organizations may hope for good "followership" (teamwork) skills, while rewarding only leadership (individual) skills. Employees learn to value and demonstrate leadership skills to the extinction of followership skills. To these employees, leading means making decisions and providing direction; following means mindless obedience. In the complex, ever-changing, interdependent, systemic business environment reality we now live in, our survival demands that we become as adept at following others as we are at getting them to follow us.

## Bringing It Home
Our organization encourages and hopes for a high level of teamwork. Great

teamwork is in the best interest of the organization and the families served. We understand that teams operating in the culture and context of a non-hierarchical, high-involvement, team-based organization are more likely to be successful. They know that teams need a common mission and purpose, clear goals, genuine authority, administrative support, skill diversity, adequate resources, and effective leadership in order to be successful. The work environment in our organization does contain these essential elements.

We take measures to ensure that individuals are good team members and do not focus only on their individual performance, such as including measures of their contributions to the team in their individual performance appraisal. We use a 360-degree appraisal because the directors know that the best source of data on an individual's contribution to the team is another member of the team (more about 360-degree appraisals in chapter 9). "Team members can be asked to rate each other on teamwork, cooperation, and contribution, and this rating, in turn, can have an impact on the level of individual rewards that employees receive" (Lawler, 1992, p. 198). We encourage members of the team to single out individuals from a team for special recognition if they have been particularly valuable team members.

The following item is extracted from our caregiver performance standards.

> Works well with other staff members to meet the needs of the children. Examples: Checks with other staff to make sure all children are supervised; is flexible about his/her roles; helps other staff out as needed; communicates with other staff in a way that role models cooperation, teamwork, cooperation, caring, and effective interaction; notices and responds supportively to non-verbal cues; shows caring and consideration for other staff in matters of punctuality and attendance; shows respect when discussing differences and solving problems; and shares concerns about children, the staff, and the program with the team.

## Conclusion
Eighteen hundred American workers ranked the following items more highly than pay as major motivators: recognition of the importance of personal and

family time, organizational direction, opportunities for personal growth, ability to challenge the way things are done, satisfaction from everyday work, and participation in planning and organizational change (Osland, et al, 2001). Hopefully we gave you enough examples to convince you this is true. We also hope we've given you enough good ideas to influence individuals!

## Discussion Questions

1. How does your team view staff learning? What systemic changes can you predict will result from team learning? If your whole team learns more about _____, it will result in _____, which will lead to _____, and _____.

2. Think about your day-to-day work environment. What does it look and sound like? Is pleasure a part of the culture of your organization? Is laughter frequent?

3. How often do you provide sincere, spontaneous acknowledgment to your staff? How often does your boss provide you with positive feedback? Do you think more genuine and specific acknowledgment and feedback would affect your own motivation?

4. Think about a typical task you ask your staff to do or a task that you wish your staff would do more of. How could you frame the work like we have framed each chapter? The work can be the whole job or individual tasks. Make sure the frame answers the question "what's in it for me?" (WIIFM).

5. What is rewarded in your organization? How? Do you see examples of rewarding A while hoping for B?

## Reference Notes

Deci, E. (1975). *Intrinsic motivation*. New York: Plenum.

Hitz, R., & Driscoll, A. (1988). Praise or encouragement? New insights into praise: Implications for early childhood teachers. *Young Children*, July 1988. 6–13.
Jensen, E. (1998). *Teaching with the brain in mind*. Alexandria, VA: Association for Supervision and Curriculum Development.

Kohn, A. (1999). *Punished by rewards: The trouble with gold stars, incentive plans, A's, praise, and other bribes*. Boston: Houghton Mifflin Company.

Kouzes, J., & Posner, B. (1995). The leadership challenge: *How to keep getting extraordinary things done in organizations*. San Francisco: Jossey-Bass.

Lawler, E. (1992). *The ultimate advantage: Creating the high-involvement organization*. San Francisco: Jossey-Bass Publishers.

Lipnack, J., & Stamps, J. (2001). Virtual teams: The new way to work.

Osland, J., Kolb, D., & Rubin, I. (2001). *Organizational behavior: An experiential approach*. Upper Saddle River, NJ: Prentice Hall.

Rolls, J. (1995). The transformational leader: The wellspring of the learning organization. In S. Chawla & J. Renesch (Eds.), *Learning Organizations* (p. 11–45). Portland, OR: Productivity Press.

Smith, D. (1996). The following part of leading. In F. Hesselbein, M. Goldsmith, & R Beckhard. (Eds.), The leader of the future. (p. 199–207). San Francisco: Jossey-Bass Publishers.

# Chapter 8: Making Variety Stew

*Variety is the spice of life.*

*Accomplishments have no color.*
*—Leontyne Price*

*I see your true colors shining through…beautiful like a rainbow.*
*—Phil Collins*

## Introduction
*It's great to work with somebody who wants to do things differently.*
*—Keith Bellows*

Mike has learned a lot about the value of diversity. This is his story. When I first became a supervisor, diversity was a challenge for me. I was intimidated by people who were not "like me" and felt that it was easy to "lead" people who were similar to me and thought like I did. I believed people who shared my viewpoints and personality styles were easier to work with. I didn't consciously discriminate against anyone based on their ethnicity, gender, or age, but I hired based on my first impressions and people who were the most like me made the best first impression on me.

Eventually I discovered that an organization full of people who were all like me was boring and didn't bring anything new to the table. I began to have more fun meeting and working with people who had different viewpoints. I grew and learned more from the people who had different experiences and different perspectives than my own.

Diverse people challenged my own theories—sometimes affirming them, and sometimes changing them. I was forced to get better at dialog. When someone says something that I disagree with, my natural reaction is to become defensive and start arguing. I try to sell my own viewpoints without listening to the other person. I am learning that I can save a lot of energy and relationships when I dialog instead of argue. By working with people who had unique outlooks and opinions, I learned to be a better leader. I learned that diversity allows for more innovation and creativity. A variety of people with different perspectives working on a problem create more potential solutions and better overall solving results. The children we work with are diverse, so having a diverse "stew" of people on my team creates stronger relationships.

This chapter is about diversity. Most of the books I have read on diversity are well-intentioned, but void of an open and honest examination of reality. They are filled with sometimes patronizing and often infantile discussions about the ethical necessity to "tolerate" diversity. They spoon feed warm and fuzzy theories about the moral correctness of primarily ethnic and gender diversity, encourage hiring based on underrepresented groups in organizations, and push for "color blind" practices—to treat everyone the same regardless of their unique traits and to be tolerant of their differences.

It is a message of "just do it" and then join hands and sing "Kumbaya" or "We are the World" and all will be well with your organization. We have attempted to offer a theory that is not a politically-correct bowl of mush, but an honest and thoughtful discussion about diversity. We are aware that we might offend people who are sensitive about diversity, we know we might step on toes, but our hope is that more good than harm will come from this open and possibly politically incorrect discussion of diversity. It is not just about ethnic diversity, but about diversity of:

- skin tones,
- gender,
- age,
- intelligences and learning styles,
- and personality styles.

We want the people on our team to share our values and our objectives, but that is the only category where we want complete unity. It is not a belief in unity versus diversity, but unity through diversity. We do not want a melting pot of people who melt together in a homogeneous solution; rather, we want a variety stew—each ingredient retaining its identity, texture, color, and flavor—different chunks of people who are unique from each other and all of whom contribute to the unity of the stew!

## Teaching Tolerance

*We should not and cannot change all our differences. Each of us brings from our own background things which we should share. There is good in diversity.*
—Georgie Anne Geyer

You will almost never hear us use the word tolerance. We don't really care for the word when it is used in a certain way. We dislike the word tolerance when it is used to describe a sense of open-mindedness and acceptance relating to diversity philosophy or practice. To tolerate something means to put up with it, to endure it. People tolerate something that is bad, but not so bad they can't possibly stand it. I might tolerate a stone in my shoe. I might tolerate a shopping cart with a squeaky wheel. Good leaders don't tolerate diversity; they value it, encourage it, embrace it, and celebrate it.

## The Value of Diversity

*There never were in the world two opinions alike, no more than two hairs or two grains; the most universal quality is diversity.*
—Michel de Montaigne

Great leaders understand and teach the real economic value of diversity. Fostering and appreciating diversity is good for business, especially in the human service sector. Ann Morrison, who coined the term "glass ceiling" writes, "In many cases personnel costs consume at least one-half to two-thirds of an organization's budget; this is especially true for service organizations. Reducing these costs can make a big difference in profitability" (1996, p. 20). High rates of staff turnover further increase these costs. Leadership that values and appreciates diversity gives minority or "nontraditional" employees incentive to stay. High performing nontraditional managers help nontraditional employees at lower levels feel more loyalty to the company. Future-focused thinkers see that in addition to the many other benefits of celebrating diversity, savings in staff recruitment, replacement, and retraining costs make a big difference in long-term profitability.

There is also strong reason to believe that solid diversity practices result in increased productivity. People are motivated to work harder when they believe in their organization and believe that they can be successful. A diverse workforce can more readily relate to and serve a diverse client base, and therefore help the organization to be more successful. A multicultural approach has a positive effect on employees' perception of equity, which in turn affects their morale, goal setting, effort, and performance (Thompson & DiTomaso, 1988). Great leaders know that appreciating diversity in the workplace will lead to increased productivity, enhanced creativity and innovation, and higher organizational loyalty.

Training and educating all members of the organization about the importance and value of diversity is critical to the success of the leader. Training must be focused on teaching all members of the organization about the means and the need to foster diversity in the workplace. It is important to make everyone more aware of the opportunities that exist in reducing differential treatment of people based on gender or ethnicity. Awareness of attitudes, behaviors, and biases that keep diversity from truly being valued and celebrated in the workplace must be discussed. Effective leaders understand the complex human relationship systems that interact in the workplace and work to align these systems toward well-defined goals and outcomes.

## Diversity of Skin Tones

*I have a dream that my four little children will one day live in a nation where they will not be judged by the color of their skin but by the content of their character.*
*—Martin Luther King, Jr.*

One of our colleagues suggested that we include in this chapter a section on African Americans, Hispanics, Native Americans, and Asians, describing how to lead people of these diverse cultures. We do not believe this is possible. Chelsea and I are both Anglo Americans, but we were raised with VERY different sets of beliefs. My brother and I are both white males, born into the same family, same geographic location, same religion—we don't even agree about what is good for children. It is impossible to compare Hispanics and Asians or to discuss what leadership philosophies work with these different cultures—which Hispanics, which Asians? All people from the same culture are not alike.

Other white guys are not "my people." Culture is extremely complex. Just because someone shares the same skin tone does not make them alike. How people are is based on their individual personality, age, family, gender, interests, religion, economic level, social status, sexual orientation, political affiliation, where they live, where they came from. Some people are "close talkers" who get up in your face; others have a larger bubble of personal space, and to a close talker can appear "standoffish." Some people are introverts and some are more outgoing. Some people of the same skin tones are carnivores; some are vegans. Some people believe eye contact shows respect; some believe it is disrespectful. Some people smile when they meet someone new; others only smile when they are genuinely happy. Some people are fast paced; their internal metronome is set at a high rate, so pauses in conversation are uncomfortable. Others speak slowly. Some people believe in "cutting the apron strings" and toughening their children up, while others encourage interdependence.

So if people from like cultures are still so different, should we all throw up our hands and quit trying to understand cultural differences? Just treat everyone as individuals? Our message is to develop relationships with people who are different than you, and to enter into dialog with them about your differences. It's all about the relationships.

We are not proponents of affirmative action. We hire people based on the content of their character, not on their education or experience, and definitely not based on their skin tones. We do understand the importance of having a diverse staff in terms of race and ethnicity. Our standards of quality include the necessity that staff can relate to a child's cultural style and primary language, and that they share the languages and cultures of the families we serve and the communities we live in. We agree with the value and significance of this standard, but instead of recruiting and hiring based on skin tones, we seek to create customs of cultural competence within our organization that make our workplace attractive to diverse and unique people—a way of life that does not tolerate diversity, but truly values and celebrates diversity.

Some organizations have a degree of cultural destructiveness—practices which seek to denigrate and destroy other cultures, practices which are hostile to any degree of diversity. Other organizations have a measure of cultural incapacity. They don't intentionally seek to be culturally destructive, but rather they lack the capacity to successfully work with diverse clients or staff.

Other organizations promote cultural blindness. They promote and accept as true the belief that culture makes no difference and that we are all the same. They endorse "color blind" policies that encourage leaders to treat everyone the same regardless of gender, race, or ethnicity. I recently heard a white colleague telling an African American colleague that she never noticed her skin color and didn't think of her as "black" because she just doesn't see the color in people. Personally, I think that is a ridiculous statement. Proponents of "color blind" philosophies expect all populations to assimilate and adapt to the dominant culture of the organization.

Some good organizations are culturally pre-competent. There is an acceptance and respect for differences and continuing self-assessment regarding organizational culture. They work to hire unbiased employees. We try to take a step farther—advanced cultural competence. In our organization we work to create an environment and traditions that promote advanced cultural competence by holding culture in high esteem. Cultural competency is an ongoing philosophy, process, and practice that builds the capacity of organizations and individuals to understand, accept, value, and honor the unique contributions of ALL people. We advocate for cultural competence throughout our systems and seek to improve relations between cultures throughout our programs and within our community.

We seek to hire culturally competent staff who can relate to the diverse children and families we serve. Culturally competent job seekers are looking to work in organizations that value individual talents and accomplishments, rather than a homogeneous set of personality characteristics. Behavioral interviewing is a practice that helps us select people with the values that we desire in our coworkers.

## Try This: Behavioral Interviews
Traditional interviews focus on first impressions and social graces which trump actual ability and behavior. In behavioral interviewing, the focus is on what the

144

person has done in the past; the person's actions (Rasmussen, 1996). We do not hire people based primarily on their skin tone, gender, age, education, or experience, but on the content of their character. What applicants have done in the past is the best predictor of future behavior, which, more than skills or experience, is the best predictor of their future job performance and ultimately their success on the job. In traditional interviewing one might ask, "What qualifications do you have that might make you a good candidate for this job?" In behavioral interviewing we would ask a slightly different question, "What in your background particularly qualifies you to be a group leader or director?" The focus is on what they have done in the past, not on their résumé. In traditional interviewing one might ask, "What is your philosophy of behavior management?" In behavioral interviewing we would say, "Tell me about a time when you had to deal with the challenging behavior of a child. What did you do?" The focus is not on their espoused theory, but on their past behavior. In a traditional interview one might ask, "If you could change one aspect of your personality, what would it be?" Instead we would ask, "What three or four adjectives best describe your personality? Give me examples of when these traits have helped or hindered you in the performance of your job."

## Diversity of Genders

In some professions females are underrepresented. In the child care and youth development profession, males are the minority in need of recruitment. The dominance of this field by females can be illustrated by an example of something that happens at conferences of early childhood and school-age care professionals. Years ago, Mike attended his first national early childhood conference. This is his story. I had eaten something that didn't agree with me and became nauseous. I hastily walked to the bathroom to vomit! When I got to the restroom, the male icons on the signs on the restroom doors had been replaced with female icons, and there was a line of women in front of both restrooms.

I went to the stairway and climbed up one floor. Here I found the same problem. The women had commandeered the bathroom. I took the stairs down two floors—same situation. There are so many more women than men at these conferences, that many of the male restrooms are temporarily changed to female restrooms. I ended up finding a trash can I could use. The point here is that when this chapter refers to "minority" in child care, it refers to any underrepresented group including males—white males and males of color.

## Diversity of Ages

Mike began his career in leadership in this profession as a college student. This is his story. I tended to hire people who looked like me. I hired mostly young people, sometimes immature, mostly college students. As a young and inexperienced leader I was intimidated by the thought of hiring an "elder." I was taught to respect and obey my elders. I didn't think I could lead someone who was older than I. Back then, I thought the role of the leader was to be the boss who had all the answers, to observe behavior and reward it if it was desirable or punish it if it was undesirable. As I learned that my job as a leader was to be the lead learner and to support and empower those who chose to work "for" me, I became less intimidated. I found it appropriate to help and support my employees who were also my elders. I learned that as a leader I could both teach and learn from my staff regardless of their age or experience. Now that my gray hair is becoming the majority and my brown hair the minority on my head, I am the "elder"—scary!

The early childhood profession is well represented by elder professionals, but the afterschool/youth development field is characterized by a younger population. When we look at the great staff who make up our organization, we see mostly young people. We have a few people in their forties to sixties, but the majority of our staff are young. Many of our line staff are college students. One reason is that our profession doesn't pay a worthy wage at this time, not a living wage for a mature person. Worthy wages are an essential element needed to attract not only mature people, but males since in our society the male is often looked to as the major bread winner in a family. Like it or not, males, mature people, or anyone who must choose an occupation based primarily on the potential level of income that the profession can provide, will only be attracted to the child care and youth development profession if the pay is adequate.

Another reason that our profession lacks mature staff is that the work requires a high level of playfulness, energy, and continuous learning. A stereotype is a fixed and distorted generalization made about all members of a particular group—a rigid judgment which doesn't take into account the here and now. We also believe that stereotypes exist because for a certain percentage of the typified group, they are true. That's right we are saying that stereotypes are often true.

The stereotype of an "old person" is someone with a low level of energy, a low level of playfulness, and an atrophied sense of learning—"you can't teach an old dog new tricks." We don't pretend this stereotype doesn't exist; we talk about it openly and honestly.

We don't discriminate based on age. We do discriminate based on character and personality issues including energy level, playfulness, and commitment to continuous learning. We let all applicants know what the job requires—lots of positive energy, playfulness, and learning. We don't expect the same energy level from an older staff person as we do from a twenty-one-year-old athlete. We treat everyone as individuals and maximize their unique contributions. We don't require EVERYONE to play kickball—but everyone must exude positive energy.

We don't ask an applicant's age. We do ask about their past behavior and actual experiences with children. We ask them what they have learned recently from working with kids and what they hope to learn. We see the value of maturity, years of experience, and wide breadth of knowledge that we can get in older, yet playful and teachable staff.

## Diversity of Intelligences & Learning Styles

Members of organizations bring a wealth and diversity of knowledge and experience. Within organizations there is a heterogeneous mix of backgrounds, learning styles, motivations, needs, interests, and goals. Leaders must tap into the diverse knowledge and experiences of all human beings everywhere in the organization. Diverse organizations benefit through their plurality of intellect. They have many smart people, but even better, they have many kinds of smart!

Intelligence is not a single narrowly-defined trait that can be quantified in an I.Q. test. Individuals differ in the types of intelligences they are born with and develop. One of the most thought-provoking theories of intelligence is Multiple Intelligences Theory. It was developed in 1983 by Dr. Howard Gardner, professor of education at Harvard University. It suggests that the traditional notion of intelligence, based on I.Q. testing, is far too limited. Instead, Dr. Gardner proposes eight different intelligences to account for a broader range of human potential in children and adults.

These intelligences are:
- Linguistic intelligence ("word smart")
- Logical-Mathematical intelligence ("number/reasoning smart")
- Spatial intelligence ("picture smart")
- Bodily-Kinesthetic intelligence ("body smart")
- Musical intelligence ("music smart")
- Interpersonal intelligence ("people smart")
- Intrapersonal intelligence ("self smart")
- Naturalist intelligence ("nature smart")

Gardner states, "It is of utmost importance that we recognize and nurture all of the varied human intelligences, and all of the combinations of intelligences" (1993, p. 12). If organizational leaders can mobilize the broad spectrum of human intelligences, they can more effectively address the broad range of organizational needs and problems that arise. People have different intelligences and different learning styles that they may exhibit when learning different subjects. Different people may learn best through different combinations of concrete experience, reflective observation, abstract conceptualization, or active experimentation (Osland, Kolb, & Rubin, 2001). Different people learn better through visual, verbal, or kinesthetic methods, so use all three. Successful individuals often attribute massive importance to "crystallizing experiences" where they first confronted an endeavor that fit their learning strengths and styles (Gardner, 1993).

Different people have varying learning styles. The more members of organizations understand their own learning styles, communication styles, and intelligences, the better they are at building positive and productive relationships with each other. It is important for organizational leaders to encourage people to discover their own learning and thinking styles and make them accessible to others (Kline & Saunders, 1998).

People learning alongside other people with different learning styles have the advantage of seeing new ways to activate and understand their own learning process. It is important that organizational leaders recognize that different learning preferences are alternate tools for approaching and accomplishing learning. We encourage leaders to ensure volunteer and staff training is conducted using all three modes of teaching—visual, verbal, and kinesthetic. It is crucial that organizational leaders recognize and accept as a goal the complete development and liberation of all human intelligence everywhere in their organizations (Kline & Saunders, 1998). Using all of the available brainpower, knowledge, and wisdom is one of the basic premises of an inclusive, culturally competent organization.

## Diversity of Personality Styles

*You can learn a lot from people who view the world differently than you do.*
*—Anthony J. D'Angelo*

In many child care and youth development programs, the ability to breathe—a warm body—is the primary criteria for entry-level employment. Organizations that are serious about improving performance and accomplishing their mission by empowering people must recruit the right people in the first place. Organizations must be clear about the most critical skills and attributes needed in its prospective employees. Organizations sometimes define the most critical attributes as experience with children, and behavior management skills. In our organization, we place a higher value on character traits such as initiative, adaptability, and ability to learn. We recruit staff who are diverse, not only in skin tones, gender, age, and intelligences, but in the styles of their personality.

We've experienced and studied many personality styles/profiles and methods of characterizing the unique gifts and personalities that people have: Introverts/ Extroverts, Spiritual Gifts (server, exhorter, leader, teacher), the Myers-Briggs (sensing, intuition, thinking feeling, judgment, perception) Gregorc Style Delineator (concrete, abstract, random, sequential), True Colors (blues, greens) Native American Personality Trait Medicine Wheel (visionaries, nurturers, activists, and analysts). We believe it is important to have diversity in these personality styles. People have many types of gifts and strengths and we want the power of all of these in our organization.

149

In the child care and youth development field, we look for specific characteristics in applicants that we are lacking in the team. In his book, *The Other Twenty-three Hours*, Dr. Al Trieshman describes three personality types that we have in our organization. The first is the "gatekeeper." This is the type of person who can keep track of everything—how many children there are in the program, where each child is at any given time, the names of all the children AND all the parents and guardians. This person usually likes to do the paperwork and is often seen carrying a clipboard. The second type is called the "soul searcher." This person is the warm, nurturing type who notices when children are feeling sad, scared, or lonely. This person works hard to comfort these children and makes sure everyone feels safe and happy. They notice when shoes are on the wrong feet or untied, and they often remember important events in children's lives like when grandparents are visiting. The last type is called the "activity freak." This is the person who loves to play and play hard. Children often don't care what activity this person is doing, they just know that whatever it is, it will be FUN. We specifically use these descriptions when looking to complete a team.

After determining what kind of people we need, the next step is figuring out how to attract them. We have found that placing classified ads is one of the best ways to broadcast position openings; however, it is important to word the job postings very intentionally to attract the type of applicant we have identified as wanting. Using words like, "Play games and sports! Take field trips! Make crafts! Be goofy, and be a good role model!" will likely attract activity freaks, whereas using words like "hiring loving and supportive individuals to care for school-age children" may attract the soul-searchers. "Seeking mature, responsible adults that will keep children safe" appeals to gate-keepers.

One ad we placed attracted a variety of characteristics. We took the Mary Poppins approach and asked some of the children in our program to describe the type of caregiver they would like. Here's how the ad looked:

CHILD CARE WORKERS—Work can be fun, fun, fun! Part-time. Care for children ages 6–11. Play games, make crafts, take field trips on Wednesdays! Teach social skills and community skills in a fun, caring environment. The CHILDREN in our program have a few wishes as well:

"Must be cool. Non-alcoholic. Has to play roller hockey. Must be funny. Must not have pickle breath. Has to play sports. Must like kids. Children's Choice has sweet children. Must not have a mean voice. Must be watchful and smart. Must be careful not to be rude, and have a cool car. Forget the roller hockey thing." Experience with school-age children required. M–F, 3–6 pm. Wednesday field trips, 1–6 pm. Also hiring for summer day camp jobs!

This ad did not attract a lot of gatekeepers. We did attract activity freaks and soul searchers. We also attracted applicants who were interested in working for an organization that respected children enough to ask for their input.

Another recruitment strategy to find diversity in staff is to use your current staff and families. Pay staff and parents a finder's fee if the organization hires people they refer. We printed referral cards that contained all the important information about the job and how to apply. Staff and parents write their names on the cards and hand them out to not only their friends, but to classmates and community members they meet who they think might be good with children. The applicant attaches the card to the completed application. This has continued to be our most successful and cheapest recruitment strategy to date. When we have diverse families and staff recruiting for us, we get applicants who reflect that diversity.

## Try This: Thinking Sanctuaries

Make your workplace safe for thinking, and you make it safe for diversity. One way to do this is to give permission to make mistakes. Another is to keep an open mind. Carefully and intentionally explain to the people on the team that your organization needs diversity of thought to learn and grow and thrive. Request that the members of your team express their disagreement with you if they have a different opinion. When someone expresses an opinion or has an idea that you disagree with, resist the urge to "fire hose" them. Fire hosing is when someone has an opinion or idea and someone on the team (often someone with more "power") extinguishes the idea by listing all of the reasons why it is incorrect or won't work. Replace the word "but" with "and" or "if." Don't say, "That's a good idea, BUT we can't afford it." Instead, say, "That's a good idea, AND it might work, IF you can find a way to afford it." Keep an open mind and you'll get more brains working for you!

## Try This: Celebrate

Don't tolerate diversity—CELEBRATE IT! We have an expression: "It is ALL about the relationships!" When it comes to getting and truly celebrating diversity this is paramount. We incorporate relationship-building activities into all of our meeting and training events—name games, get-to-know-you games, communication exercises, and guided discussions about personal issues. The better we know each other, the better we understand each other, the more value we get out of our diversity. I encourage leaders to celebrate with staff and with families. In many organizations celebrations are forbidden out of a misguided fear of offending someone. During the winter holiday season, we can't wish someone a Merry Christmas without worrying about offending someone, and we can use a tree as a decoration only if it does not have a star or angel on top. I think this is political correctness gone wrong.

We say allow your staff and children to celebrate anything they celebrate at home. Celebrate Black History Month, Hispanic Heritage Month, Asian Pacific Islander Month, Hanukah, Christmas, Kwanzaa. Celebrate No-Name-Calling Week, Flag Day, Earth Day, Citizenship Day, and Restless Leg Syndrome Awareness Day. Okay, we made that last one up. Definitely celebrate Boss's Appreciation Day! Celebrate it and then have discussions about it. Provide people with the opportunity to educate each other and talk about their differences and similarities. The point is to let them celebrate what is important to them. And if their beliefs include NOT celebrating anything your program chooses to celebrate…then celebrate that child's right to choose to opt out. "Celebration by Choice!" This is advanced cultural competency in action. It brings diversity out in the open to be truly celebrated.

## Try This: Family Trees

I see many strange and failed attempts to portray diversity in the décor of child care environments. Staff purchase pictures of kids with different skin tones wearing costumes and performing stereotypic actions—a Mexican kid wearing a sombrero leaning up against a cactus taking a siesta, or a Japanese kid wearing a kimono and flying a carp kite. Don't buy that garbage that reinforces stereotypes in a touristic approach to diversity. In our programs we put up a family tree—a picture of a tree that is a place where kids and staff can post pictures of their family (however they define their family).

152

Defining a family as a mother, father, and child it not fair to children who do not have a "traditional nuclear family." Encourage children to post images of their family, no matter how they define their family. When they put up portraits, snapshots, or family vacation pictures, it affirms the importance of family. It guarantees that your décor reflects the diversity of your community because it IS your community. It shows your love of diversity in a real way.

## Try This: Tell Your Story

We use games like these to get people talking about themselves. They help us to understand and discuss our similarities and differences.

### Personalized Name Tags

Have each person create a nametag or coat of arms that includes symbols or pictures that represent something he or she feels good about. Then go around the room and share names and what each person is proud of.

### Precious Objects

Tell participants to choose something important to them from among the items they have with them—something that says something about them. Once everyone has chosen, tell them to pair up with someone they don't know well, without talking. Have them exchange objects and decide who will be the talker (who will tell why the object is important to them and what it says about them) and who will be the listener (who will listen, nothing more). Afterward ask, "What if I told you that the other person would be holding your object until the end of the day? How would you feel? What if I told you that when you get your object back it won't be quite the same because the other person would have formed a relationship with it?" Usually there is a wave of emotions. Make the point that it is a little like parents leaving a child in our program with a teacher they don't know very well. This can generate a good discussion about cultural differences (Shareef & Gonzalez-Mena, 2008).

### Two Truths and a Lie

Each person thinks of two things that are true (and interesting) about themselves and one thing that is not true. Then each person tells their list to the others as if they are all true. The team tries to guess which one is a lie.

**Uncommon Commonalities**

Split into teams of three or four. Have each group find the most uncommon thing they all have in common—the weirdest thing that they all have in common.

**Where You From? Where You Been?**

Use a rope to create a map of the city, county, state, or country you are from (or a place you have recently traveled to), and tell us something about that place (from Jim Cain, see Helpful Resources).

**Who are You ?**

Ask the team to brainstorm a list of questions they would want to know about a person (What is your favorite TV show? What is your most embarrassing moment? Who are your heroes?). Narrow down the list to two or three questions that the team likes the best. Allow the team to mingle and ask the questions and record (or remember) the answers.

## Try This: Suggestion Circle

*The golden rule of conduct is mutual toleration, seeing that we will never all think alike and we shall always see Truth in fragment and from different points of vision.*
*—Mahatma Gandhi*

Diversity of ideas is a powerful resource. It leads to better problem solving. The next time someone on your team asks for some help with ideas to solve a problem or a suggestion, try a suggestion circle to maximize the diversity of thought.

Here's how it works.
1. Everyone stands up. This keeps people from expounding endlessly on their suggestions.
2. Designate one person to write down all of the suggestions, so the person asking for help can pay attention, and still have a record of ideas to consider.
3. Instruct the person asking for help to again rephrase the problem or the request for ideas, so that everyone understands the issue.
4. Tell the person who asked for help that because the quantity of ideas is the goal, they may only respond to suggestions offered with ONLY two words: "thank you."

5. By saying only "thank you." The person asking for help will not run the risk of "fire-hosing" people's ideas and unintentionally limiting creativity. Even if the person has already tried the suggestion or knows it won't work: "thank you."
6. When the brainstorming is complete, give the person requesting help the list of suggestions, so he or she can consider them all in private and decide what, if any, suggestions to take.

## Bringing It Home

*Our creator rejoices in diversity and variety. Any observation of our abundant earth and its incredibly different life-forms proves this.*
—Robyn Knibbe

Ann Morrison, coauthor of Breaking the Glass Ceiling, describes five steps that can help managers organize and answer the questions that need to be addressed in creating and carrying out a diversity plan. These steps are:
1. Discover diversity problems in your organization.
2. Strengthen top-management commitment.
3. Choose solutions that fit a balanced strategy.
4. Demand results and revisit the goals.
5. Use building blocks to maintain momentum.

She suggests the importance of using a team or task force to gather information regarding diversity problems within the organization because having adequate representation is essential to insure an impartial perspective. She also emphasizes that diversity must become a pervasive part of the culture if the commitment is to continue beyond one CEO or one manager (1996).

Her research revealed common characteristic tools and practices that organizations report using as part of their diversity efforts: The top management of the organization uses influence to promote diversity and accountability for diversity. There is a targeted recruitment of non-traditional workers for entry-level positions. Organizations use internal advocacy forces or task forces to address diversity issues. There is an emphasis on equal employment opportunity statistics or personnel profiles. There is an incorporation of diversity into performance evaluations or goals. There is targeting of non-traditional employees in the management succession process, and a revision of promotion criteria and the decision-making process to reflect diversity goals (1996).

Effective leaders must make efforts to recruit staff members who share the languages and cultures of the families they serve, and the communities they live in. They must intentionally make efforts to recruit staff members who can relate to a child's cultural style and primary language. All recruited staff members must have the skills and abilities needed to be a productive member of the organization. Remember that hiring for diversity does not mean hiring or promoting members of covered groups who are less qualified than the dominant group in their profession.

Effective leaders must work to increase job satisfaction and decrease turnover of all employees. When minority employees succeed and remain with the organization, they inspire new minority employees to perform well and to stay. All employees must experience a welcoming orientation process designed to make them comfortable and successful in the beginning stages of employment. All employees must have the opportunity for professional development programs to improve their skills and qualify them for promotions. Being included in a professional development, for example, may motivate non-traditional employees to remain with an organization and to perform to their best ability because they see further opportunities for themselves (Morrison, 1996).

A successful, more experienced employee should mentor all new employees. "Mentors can buffer minorities from adverse forces in the organization, and help them navigate through the challenging and changing political terrain" (Ragins, Townsend, & Mattis, 2001). Involving all employees in all orientation, training, development, and mentoring programs will foster a sense of unity within the organization, and will provide opportunities for people of different ethnicities and genders to develop communication and teamwork skills together.

Leaders can do many things to foster appreciation for diversity. Effective leaders must challenge people who make prejudiced comments or use stereotypes to describe people, and take disciplinary action to stop any harassment. Leaders must set an example in their behavior of a celebration of diversity. Leaders will encourage respect for individual differences, and promote understanding of different beliefs and traditions. Leaders will explain the many benefits of diversity for the small teams and the organization as a whole, and use their influence to make the celebration of diversity a pervasive part of the culture of the organization.

The National AfterSchool Association developed The NAA Standards for Quality School-Age Care. These standards are the nationally recognized standards, the accepted norm, and the minimal definition of a quality school-age care program in the United States. There are 144 quality standards in the NAA Standards for Quality School-Age Care. School-age care programs that comply with all of the 144 standards of quality are eligible for accreditation. Four of these standards address diversity:
1. Staff can relate to a child's cultural style and primary language.
2. Staff share the languages and cultures of the families they serve, and the communities they live in.
3. Activities reflect the languages and cultures of the families served.
4. Staff plan activities that will reflect the cultures of the families in the program and the broad diversity of human experience (Roman, 1998).

According to the *Code of Ethics for School-Age Care*, in quality school-age care programs, issues of diversity and sensitivity are championed by staff and children (Charron, 1997). One of the developmental assets, which predict positive developmental outcomes for school-age children, is the development of cultural competence, having knowledge of and comfort with people of different cultural/racial/ethnic backgrounds (Leffert, Benson, & Roehlkepartain, 1997).

In our book *Best Practices for School-Age Child Care*, we say that the following should be consistently and readily observable in the human relationships of the child care and youth development program.
1. The program makes every attempt to communicate with family members in their own language about their child's growth and development.
2. The staff members accept and respect each family's definition of family composition, ethnicity, culture, roles, and relationships.
3. The staff members model positive values, reflect cultural and gender diversity, and are philosophically aligned with the program goals and desired results.

4. The adults know the interests, talents, abilities, cultures, and languages of children in the program.
5. The adults can relate to the children's cultural style and primary language.
6. The adults respond to the range of diverse children with understanding and inclusion, varying the approaches they use to facilitate learning and development.
7. The adults respond to each child with respect, acceptance, and comfort, regardless of gender, socioeconomic status, race, ethnicity, ability, religion, or family background.
8. The children develop cultural competence, knowledge of, and comfort with people of different cultural, racial, or ethnic backgrounds.
9. The staff members share the languages and cultures of the families they serve (Ashcraft, 2001).

The mission of our organization is to facilitate the positive development of children. This includes teaching them social and cultural competencies, how to make friends, how to resolve problems, how to relate to people of different cultures, and how to communicate their thoughts and emotions. The children in the programs are diverse. It is important to our mission that the caregivers can relate to the culture and languages of the children. It is important that the families can relate to the staff. The activities, the environment, and the staff need to reflect the diversity of the families in the organization in order to accomplish the mission.

In order to teach these social competencies, all of the caregivers and administrators in the organization must possess these competencies and be experts in demonstrating and teaching these them. The significance of diversity issues is paramount to the mission. Cultural diversity has always been fully incorporated into the real life of the organization. The staff team is like a family. They work, plan, strategize, create, argue, play, laugh, and sometimes cry together. Everything is not perfect in the organization, but diversity has been something that makes the organization richer. When different people enter the organization, especially people of different backgrounds, everyone gains in diversity of perspective and in increase of their knowledge base.

## Conclusion

*If we cannot end now our differences, at least we can help make the world safe for diversity.*
—John F. Kennedy

Many advocates of diversity encourage organizations to treat all of their employees the same way—a level playing field, "color-blind and gender-blind." We do not believe that you should treat all people the same! People are different— that is the point of diversity, so why would you spend so much time creating a diverse team and then treat everyone the same? We have all heard of the golden rule, "Treat others the same way YOU want to be treated." Diversity has taught me that EVERYONE doesn't want to be treated the same way I want to be treated. The new rule for a culturally competent organization is the platinum rule: "Treat others the way THEY want to be treated." Talk about the differences people have. Don't be afraid of it. Ask people how they like to receive feedback. Ask them about their beliefs, styles, and preferences. Ask them how they handle conflict. Really get to know your diverse team and then treat them as individuals.

Final point about diversity: our field is diverse in terms of what we believe is in the best interest of children. The afterschool profession includes people from the 21st Century Community Learning Centers paradigm, which stresses academics; other programs are recreation based and stress the need for a break from academics. The quality school-age child care model stresses choice, autonomy, and child-directed activities. In early childhood some educators stress learning through play, while others stress academically challenging very young children.

Some provide early childhood education in schools, some in child care centers, and some advocate for home-based care. Our point is that there is plenty of room in our field for variety of perspectives, culturally shaped and otherwise. There is not only one way to make a friend, one way to make a decision, or one way to educate a child. If you follow just your own ideas about what's good and right for children, even based on your training and education in child development, you may be doing a disservice to children of families who disagree with you. Our message is to understand yourself, become clear about your own values and goals, and define what you believe in. Have a bottom line, but be flexible and truly dialog, interact, and listen to the perspectives of others.

## Discussion Questions

1. You know the importance of diversity, of recruiting staff who look like and can relate to the diverse populations you serve. What recruitment strategies have you implemented that have been successful in recruiting diverse staff?

2. Have you "fire hosed" anyone lately? When your followers offer a "new" idea that you have tried in the past, do you quickly point out that you've already "been there, done that," or do you let them speak and ask questions to help them formulate ways that their ideas could possibly work better than past attempts?

3. When a problem happens in your organization, do you try to identify who caused the problem rather than identify what systems contributed to the problem? Think of a recurring problem you experience. Now try to identify the systemic causes for the problem—focus on the systems, not the symptoms!

4. Do you like working with people who think and act like you do? What are some advantages and disadvantages to working with people who think and behave like you do?

5. Think of the last time you fired someone. The reason most likely was negative behavior rather than lack of a skill—an issue of values more than performance. Now think back to when you interviewed that person. What questions did you ask in the interview that screened for these behaviors?

6. Think of a top performer in your organization. What behaviors or values make them a good member of your team? Clarifying exactly what makes for an outstanding employee and will help you in making good hires in the future. What questions can you ask in an interview that will help you screen for these traits?

## Helpful Resources
Download the handout to Games that Build Community Fast at www.childrens-choice.org/training.html

Gardner, H. (1993). *Multiple intelligences: the theory in practice.* New York: Basic Books.

Myers-Briggs Type Indicator® (MBTI) personality inventory utilizes the theory of psychological types described by C. G. Jung.
www.myersbriggs.org

Gregorc Associates, Mind Styles, and the Gregorc Style Delineator.
www.gregorc.com

*Teamwork & Teamplay,* 1998, by Jim Cain and Barry Jolliff, Kendall Hunt Publishers, Dubuque, Iowa is 419 pages of portable adventure-based activities, equipment, resources, and references. Download a sample of thirty activities at www.teamworkandteamplay.com

## Reference Notes

Adler, L. (1998). *Hire with your head: A rational way to make a gut decision.*

Brethower, D. & Smalley, K. (1998). P*erformance-based instruction: Linking training to business results.* San Francisco: Jossey-Bass/Pheiffer.

Charron, L. (Ed.). (2001). *Code of ethics for school-age care.* (SAC Monograph No. 1). St. Paul, MN: Concordia University, Concordia School of Human Services.

Cross, T. (1988). *Cultural competence continuum. Focal point, the bulletin of the research and training center on family support ant children's mental health.* Portland, OR: Portland State University.

DeLuca, M. & DeLuca, N. (2001). *More best answers to the 201 most frequently asked interview questions.*

Gonzalez-Mena, J. (2008). *Diversity in Early care and education: Honoring differences.* New York: McGraw Hill.

Kline, P., & Saunders, B. (1998). *Ten steps to a learning organization.* Arlington, VA: Great Ocean Publishers.

Leffert, N., Benson, P., & Roehlkepartain, J. (1997). *Starting out right: Developmental assets for children.* Minneapolis, MN: Search Institute.

Morrison, A. (1996). *The new leaders: Leadership diversity in America.* San Francisco: Jossey-Bass Publishers.

Ollhoff, J. & Walcheski, M. (2002). *Stepping in wholes: Introduction to complex systems.* Eden Prairie, MN: Sparrow Media Group, Inc.

Raggins, B., Tonwsend, B., & Mattis, M. (2001). Gender gap in the executive suite: CEO's and female executives report on breaking the glass ceiling. In J. Osland, D. Kolb, & I. Rubin. (Eds.), *The organizational behavior reader.* (p. 211–226). Upper Saddle River, NJ: Prentice Hall.

Rasmussen, T. (1996). The ASTD *Trainer's Sourcebook: Diversity.*

Roman, J. (Ed.). (1998). *The NSACA standards for quality school-age care.* Boston, MA: National School-Age Care Alliance.

Shareef, I., & Gonzalez-Mena, J. (2008). *Practice in building bridges: Companion resource to diversity in early care and education.* Washington DC: National Association for the Education of Young Children.

Trieshman, A. E., Whittaker, J. K. & Brendtro, L. K. (1969). *The other twenty-three hours: child care work with emotionally disturbed children in a therapeutic milieu.* New York: Aldine de Gruyer.

# Chapter 9: Tackling Turnover

*By working faithfully eight hours a day, you may eventually get to be a boss and work twelve hours a day.*
—*Robert Frost*

*Modern cynics and skeptics…see no harm in paying those to whom they entrust the minds of their children a smaller wage than is paid to those to whom they entrust the care of their plumbing.*
—*John F. Kennedy*

*Take this job and shove it. I ain't workin' here no more!*
—*David Allan Coe*

## Introduction

Child development experts and advocates share the strong opinion that youth will be best served by school-age care practitioners who are well-trained, well-compensated, and likely to remain in their jobs (National Institute on Out-of-School Time (NIOST), 2001b). If you cannot retain the employees that you recruit, you will be swimming upstream, fighting a very difficult battle. If you can't keep them, there will be no one to lead. We would imagine this story is all too familiar to most directors. Unfortunately, there is not an easy fix to staff turnover. The good news is that you can greatly reduce turnover by intentionally using specific strategies throughout the entire hiring process from recruitment of applicants to staff development.

Our organization has a low rate of turnover. Last year it was about 20 percent. In the past twelve years, everyone who voluntarily left our organization either changed career fields or moved out of town. In our city of more than five hundred thousand people no one has quit for a better local job in child care.

The best way to retain staff is to do the things we have discussed in this book so far. Creating a Learning Organization, empowering, and coaching your staff are the biggest and most powerful tools to use. This chapter will include more specific strategies that will help you reduce turnover.

It is increasingly difficult to maintain staffing in child care organizations, especially those that care for school-age children. The field of school-age care is plagued by an unacceptably high rate of staff turnover that is detrimental to program quality and contrary to the best interests of the children. This high rate is due to the fact that the school-age care profession offers very low compensation, and lacks a professional development system, a core body of knowledge, a career matrix, and a system of training.

Annual turnover rates average about 50 percent, and are as high as 300 percent in some programs (Vandenbergh & Locklear, 2000). This means that each position gets filled three times in one year! Elementary school principals from all around the country have reported that recruiting and retaining caregivers was one of the biggest challenges facing their school-age care programs (National Association of Elementary School Principals, 2001). A 2001 study found a highest average mean turnover rate of 32 percent for aides in school-age care programs compared to a turnover rate of 9 percent for public school teachers (Chase, 2001).

## Quality

The workforce is in a state of crisis plagued by chronic staff turnover, which is crippling the quality of many programs (NIOST, 2001b). Research has shown that the school-age care profession's ability to reach established standards of quality has been compromised by turnover rates that have more than doubled over the last two decades (NIOST, 2001a). One of the greatest reasons for poor-quality afterschool programs include high turnover due to poor wages and compensation (U.S. Department of Education, 1998).

High turnover is the antithesis of quality child care management. "People working in child care describe turnover as a time sponge, an energy drain, or even a plague. Some centers go out of business when turnover gets too high" (Whitebook & Bellm, 1999). School-age child care programs are simultaneously experiencing an accelerated rate of growth and grappling with high staff turnover; therefore, staying fully staffed has become a frustrating exercise of developing the skills of staff members, only to see them leave for higher-paying, full-time work (NIOST, 2001b).

Turnover of caregivers in school-age care programs is a major indicator of quality. The National Child Care Staffing Study revealed that children in centers with high turnover spent less time engaged in social activities and were found to build vocabulary at slower rates than those in more stable settings (Whitebook, Howes, & Phillips, 1990; Howes, Phillips, & Whitebook, 1992). Children in higher-quality programs which were associated with low turnover rates had better language and pre-math skills, had more positive self-concepts, engaged in better relationships with their teachers, and demonstrated more advanced social competencies (Helburn, 1995).

Staff turnover and program quality are issues that together create systems that can work to improve or worsen themselves. Poor-quality programs are associated with more job stress and less job satisfaction, which contribute to higher staff turnover. Higher staff turnover drives program quality further down, which again increases staff turnover. Conversely, high-quality programs are associated with happy and satisfied staff. These satisfied staff members remain in these quality programs longer, and this low turnover rate creates an even higher-quality program.

## Try This: Make a Top Ten for Recruiting

Before you can hire and retain the people you want in your organization, you'll need to get some people interested in working with you. Create a David Letterman-style "Top Ten List." Actually we made ours a Top Eleven list for a little novelty. Why would someone want to work in your organization? Put it on your Web site, on your application, on t-shirts, on the back of business cards. Here is our list. Feel free to borrow from it.

Top ELEVEN Reasons to JOIN THE Children's Choice TEAM
1. Competitive pay and benefits.
2. Helping kids learn and develop is a great gig.
3. Empowerment: all staff have a role in decision making.
4. Happy and fun-loving coworkers.
5. Supportive supervisors.
6. We all LEARN together.
7. Valuable experience.
8. Opportunities to make a real difference.

9. Hugs, laughs, and great memories are all in a day's work!

10. Opportunities for advancement.

11. We get paid to have FUN!

## Hiring Process

Keeping good staff members requires you to first find the staff members you want to keep. We began this book discussing the need to create a compelling vision— charting the course. In his best-selling book *Good to Great*, Jim Collins found through extensive research of great organizations something that his research team did not expect to find. They expected that good-to-great leaders would begin by setting a vision and strategy, but found instead that they first got the right people "on the bus, the wrong people off the bus, and the right people in the right seats." They didn't first decide where to drive the bus and then get people to drive it there (2001).

People who accept a job with our organization do so because of the people who work here more often than because of a written statement of our mission or vision. It's all about the relationships! They say, "Hey, I got on this bus because of who else is on it; if we need to alter course, fine with me."

Great vision without great people is irrelevant. If you get the right people on the bus, they don't need to be controlled or even motivated to produce great results. In our organization we are ALWAYS looking for great people. We hire outstanding people whenever and wherever we find them. If we find someone great, but we have no open positions, we'll create a new position just to get the person onboard.

This is our hiring process.

Step 1: Fill out and submit employment application

Step 2: Interview may be granted based on application

Step 3: Secondary interview (sometimes)

Step 4: Background check

Step 5: Job offer

Step 6: Orientation = Onboarding

Use your application as the first interview. Designing your application process to identify the exact characteristics you are looking for in an applicant will help identify staff members who want to stay with your organization longer and will help reduce the time you spend on this task.

Use the application as a tool to weed out the people you are not interested in hiring. Typical applications ask only basic information. Add more probing questions to find out if the applicants have the characteristics you identified in the recruitment section. Scenarios and open-ended questions work great. Another advantage to having a longer, more thought provoking application is that it may detract some applicants from filling it out. That is great. Our application has been referred to as a "book." It usually takes applicants about an hour to complete it and many don't even return it. Because of this, we spend less time reading through unqualified applicants, and the applications we do get returned are more likely from people we are interested in hiring. More than likely, people who can't even complete the application will not be willing to do the hard work it requires to care for children.

Review the applications received and choose the ones with answers that most consistently match the qualities you are searching for in employees. Setting up interviews so at least two people can attend is vital. First, it allows the interviewers to compare notes and communicate their perceptions of the applicant.

Second, and most importantly, it allows others to feel valued for their opinions. An open invitation should be given to all staff members when conducting interviews for all positions within the organization. Teach those who do attend the interview the correct and legal interviewing procedures. Also teach them the flow of an interview. Each organization will have its own questions and style. We like to organize our interviews into three main parts: working with children, working with parents, and working with coworkers and supervisors. We ask open-ended questions and give "what would you do" scenarios pertaining to each section. We ask how they have handled specific situations in the past. A novice interviewer is helped by this routine because he or she knows what kind of questions to ask and when. A simple prompting such as "Does anyone have any more kid questions, or should we move on to parents?" is given by the lead interviewer.

At the end of the interview, after the applicant has left, discuss his or her strengths and weaknesses. Start with the newest employee and work around the group to the most experienced one. This allows newer, less confident employees the chance to be heard without feeling intimidated to participate. This discussion serves not just to improve the hiring process, but also as training to the current staff who attended. They get to understand what qualities and skills are important when employed by the organization.

Newer employees start not by giving thumbs-up or thumbs-down opinions, but by listing some of the applicant's strengths and weaknesses. Strengths might include genuine caring about children, realistic expectations about the behavior of children, understanding of developmental appropriateness, unique interests which can be folded into the curriculum, a playful attitude, a hunger for learning, a positive attitude, a philosophy about development that is a "good fit" with our mission, or an understanding of quality standards. Weaknesses may include a lack of any of the strengths we listed. When we identify a deficit of some kind we ask ourselves, "Is this a skill deficit—something that can be learned, or is this a values deficit—a character flaw?" If we believe it is a skill deficit, we ask ourselves, "Is this person a sponge for learning?"

In a recent interview we asked an applicant what qualified her to be considered for this position. She said, "I've worked in early childhood. I ran my own family home care program. I've worked in juvenile justice. I've done it all. I know everything there is to know about working with children." This is an example of an unspongy response. We did not hire her. We don't hire based on education or experience, but on attitude—a positive and professional attitude and desire to learn and continually improve one's day-to-day practice. If we are in doubt, we don't hire. We keep looking.

Current staff members who participate in these interviews will be more willing to look at their own skills and qualities to make sure they are living up to the organizations' expectations. They will be more encouraged to improve their own performance. A third benefit from this process is that the participants feel empowered because they get to help choose who will work with them. Yes, this process has a much higher cost than interviewing an applicant alone since we are paying everyone sitting around the table. However, this process combines many tasks at the same time—hiring, training, inspiring, motivating, empowering—and results in a bigger bang for the buck.

Recently an applicant during a second interview commented that when he went home after his first interview he thought about how impressed he was with the questions that were asked of him. He really hoped we would hire him because he wanted to work for an organization that places such a high value on children that it would take these great measures to find good people to work with them.

## Onboarding

After everyone has decided that the applicant is a good match for the organization, and the job offer has been made, the welcoming to the organization begins. Getting the right people onboard correctly reduces turnover. Beginning to work for an organization like ours is a different experience than in other organizations. Sometimes it takes some getting used to. New staff members may expect and even feel more comfortable being told what to do and how to do it. It takes a lot of orientation to help new people understand that our expectations are different.

Because members of our organization are expected to think creatively and with a team to understand the big picture, better solve problems, and work under less supervision, it is vital that they receive information to understand the expectations or the boundaries that we discussed earlier. Think of it like giving students the answers to the final at the beginning of the semester. The job description as well as the performance evaluation tool should be given at this time. Show them what is expected of them and what the standards are that they are expected to meet right at the beginning of their employment.

It is important that members of our organization are able to see the big picture and understand how they work within the flow of the system. In order to understand this, they must be given more information than just policies and procedures. Policies and procedures are important, but teaching employees how to think for themselves and be good at solving problems is more important and must start immediately. Orientation should be used to help new employees understand their job better as well as how to fit into this new environment. We have continually improved our orientation process over the years and it now has three parts. The first part takes place on the first day the new employee is at the site. Instead of working with the children, new hires are given a tour by other staff members of where everything is and why it is needed. They are expected to keep track of this tour with a check list they are given. This day is completed with a scavenger hunt. New staff members are asked a variety of questions that can only be answered by knowing where to receive that information—sometimes they need to ask another staff member a question, other times they need to talk with a child or two—helping to begin to develop these important relationships. This is a pop quiz of sorts, but in a more fun, memorable way. The second part of the orientation takes place over the next five days.

Each of the five days is broken down into different tasks. The first day is spent on their own, reading all the materials they are given when hired. This includes things like the parent manual, the staff manual, and the NAA standards. The next four days are spent getting to know the kids and the families. They spend their time introducing themselves and remembering names. They also spend time looking through each child's registration file to learn more about allergies, medications, and special needs. They watch the YouTube Children's Choice Parent Orientation Videos. This five-day orientation is a long process and sometimes painful if the program is in desperate need of a staff member. But we have found that toughing it out for these few days reaps bigger rewards overall for both the team and the program.

Finally, the last part of our orientation process is a formal six-hour information session every new employee must attend. Mike leads this information session that teaches new staff members about our mission, our philosophical foundations, systems thinking, and the learning and leadership philosophies of our organization. We have found that this session is most effective when employees have had a chance to experience the program for a while first. It is easier to make connections to help create a better understanding.

## Try This: Make a Pitch
A lot of people enter the child care or youth development profession with no

thought of making a career out of it. Many of them take their first job with the perspective of it being only a steppingstone on the way to a "real job." Our profession is growing and changing. Public awareness about the importance of our profession is at an all time high. Funding is growing. There are many growing opportunities to make a career in this field. Our profession needs leaders, administrators, grant writers, professors, trainers, and consultants. Spend time in your onboarding process talking about this exciting and growing field. Make a pitch for the profession. Describe the possible career ladders that are available to make a rewarding and enjoyable career in this field.

## Try This: New Hire Scavenger Hunt

Modify our new employee scavenger hunt to make it appropriate for your use.

Welcome to our team! We have developed this as a fun way to get to know the space you will be working in and the people you will be working with. Please use the children and the staff to help you complete this scavenger hunt.

1. Find the time sheet book, put your name in it, and clock in.
2. Write a "Hi I'm New" message to everyone in the staff communication log.
3. Call the office and say you're beginning the scavenger hunt.
4. What is your site director's cell phone number?
5. Who is the President of Kids' Council?
6. What is his/her favorite thing to have for snack?
7. Who is the assistant director?
8. What is his/her favorite thing about this job?
9. What is the name of another staff member?
10. What is his/her favorite field trip to take with kids?
11. What is the name of another staff member?
12. What is his/her favorite activity to do with the kids?
13. Find the "proper handwashing" signs. How many seconds are recommended?
14. Find the activity calendar. What is happening next Wednesday?
15. Where are the dry snack items located?
16. What is the phone number for poison control?
17. Where are the adults-only craft supplies like glitter?
18. What is the second rule posted in the cafeteria?

19. What color is the copy of the accident report that the parent receives?
20. Where are the charging units for the walkie-talkies?
21. What was the date of the last fire drill?
22. Look at the posted staffing schedule. Who works on Wednesday afternoon?
23. What pieces of information on the kids' registration form does law require?
24. Who is the first child/family in the family file box?
25. Who is the last child/family in the family file box?
26. Where is the bleach and water spray bottle for disinfecting the tablecloths?
27. Where are the rags used to clean the tablecloths?
28. Where is the mop water cleaning solution?
29. Where do you record what was served for snack each day?
30. Where is the backpack with first aid supplies that goes on all field trips?
31. What color clothespin do children put by their names when they go outside?
32. What is the third step of the discipline policy?
33. What happens when a child is running in the cafeteria?
34. Please sign this scavenger hunt and attach it to your first time sheet.
35. Call Mike or Chelsea and let them know you've finished doing the scavenger hunt.

Thank you, we hope this was fun, informative and helpful!

## Worthy Wages

One of the most obvious issues tied to turnover is that of low wages. If child care/afterschool/youth development educators cannot earn a worthy living wage in school-age care, they will seek other employment. The Bureau of Labor Statistics of the U.S. Department of Labor reports mean wages for over seven hundred occupations, as surveyed by the Occupational Employment Statistics (OES) program. According to the 2004 OES survey, only seventeen occupations report having lower mean wages than child care workers. Those who earn higher wages than child care workers include service station attendants, parking lot attendants, kennel workers, tree trimmers, and food servers. On average, childcare workers earn $17,300 annually (Center for the Child Care Workforce, 2004), slightly more than the 2007 federal poverty guidelines for a family of three (U.S. Department of Health and Human Services).

The Massachusetts Recruitment and Retention Project found that low wages are still considered to be the top cause of turnover of school-age care practitioners, and recommends paying worthy wages as a strategy to reduce turnover in school-age care (NIOST, 2001a). Centers suffer from high turnover rates and are forced to retain poorly-performing personnel. The low pay of caregivers and the resulting high rates of turnover were frequently cited as major problems in the Department of Defense's child care system (Campbell, et al, 2000). Increased wages tied to increased staff competencies was a significant step that dramatically improved military child care.

The Wilder Research Center conducted a study that found turnover rates are inversely related to wages—as wages go up, practitioner turnover goes down. This research has shown that in school-age care programs, dissatisfaction with pay was the top reason for staff leaving and that competitive pay is an effective strategy to reduce turnover (Chase, 2001).

School-age care programs may never be able to pay caregivers what they are truly worth, but they must find ways to establish compensation levels that are fair and competitive in the human service industry. When caregivers and site directors are worrying and complaining about their pay, they spend less energy on improving performance and accomplishing the mission of the organization. Competitive compensation should not be viewed as a consequence of organizational success, but a prerequisite for success. Good compensation is an investment in quality programs, and that investment should start with site directors first, and caregivers second—NOT with upper-level administrators who do not work directly with the children and families and therefore do not have as much potential impact on the success of the organization.

How do you do this? Everything we discuss in this book will help you in a business sense, to have more money to use on your most important resource—your people. Hire disciplined people and then involve all of them in the budget process so they understand where the precious dollars are spent. Eliminate overhead and unnecessary costs. Eliminate bureaucratic tasks that waste time and money. If it doesn't add to quality or help you accomplish your mission, don't spend money on it. Most of us make "to do" lists. This involves making a "stop doing" list.

This must start with the leadership; you can't expect everyone to make sacrifices and exercise fiscal restraint while you sit on high and waste resources. It involves creating a culture of discipline. Be fanatically consistent about fiscal responsibility and hold yourself and everyone accountable for exercising restraint in spending. Negotiate for the best prices on what you purchase for your programs. Ask for donations. Take full advantage of volunteers. Take advantage of every funding opportunity you can find to assist you in paying a worthy wage. See the Helpful Resources section for a link to funding information.

## Work Environment

The Massachusetts Recruitment and Retention Project recommends making sure staff have a say in program management as a strategy to reduce turnover in school-age care (NIOST, 2001a). Research has shown that teambuilding, good communication, and a supportive work environment are effective strategies to reduce turnover (Chase, 2001). High-involvement organizations that empower employees to do work formerly done by administrators (planning field trips, writing curriculum, creating newsletters, etc.) allow management time to concentrate on areas that are more likely to ensure the organization's accomplishment of its mission. Time formerly used for checking up on employees and controlling their work can be spent developing new training opportunities for the staff. It also has another benefit in terms of compensation.

By developing front-line employees to exercise control formerly reserved for administrators, organizations can create more full-time jobs (with benefits) for entry-level workers, an added compensation strategy that can increase job satisfaction and productivity and simultaneously reduce staff turnover. Working in a high-involvement, empowering organization is in and of itself an element of compensation. High-involvement organizations therefore have less turnover because employees find these organizations more attractive places to work (Lawler, 1992). Another way to reduce turnover is to provide better training more often. U.S. military child care programs underwent a transformation when they increased both wages and training opportunities.

## Linked Competencies and Compensation

A report produced by the National Women's Law Center describes the transformation of the child care and school-age care programs provided by the military since the Military Child Care Act (MCCA) of 1989 (Campbell, et al, 2000). The U.S. military programs that were once called the ghetto of American child care are now acclaimed as a model for the nation. This report examines the specific ways in which the military achieved this transformation and provides lessons on how similar improvements might be made in the civilian sector.

In the past, the military did not provide adequate training for caregivers. In the transformed military child development programs caregivers now receive ongoing training and increased compensation that is linked to their training. Staff turnover, which was once as high as 300 percent, has been reduced dramatically to less than 30 percent; staff morale and professionalism have all improved.

Several steps were taken including raising caregiver compensation, linking increased wages to training, developing a comprehensive training program, and hiring training and curriculum specialists. The military thereby achieved its ultimate goal of developing a better-trained, more stable workforce.

To help civilian programs achieve the same goal, The Massachusetts Recruitment and Retention Project recommends an improvement plan that includes structural changes in management such as improved salaries, benefits, and training opportunities, which will enable programs to recruit and retain well-trained caregivers. In a technical assistance paper, *Recruiting and Retaining School-age Care Staff in Today's Challenging Climate,* the YMCA recommends that providers move staff from a casual to a committed relationship with the program by utilizing periodic salary increases and by providing opportunities to learn new skills and attend training (YMCA of the USA, 2001).

Anne Noonan, Ph.D. identifies developing an agreed-upon professional development system as a critical factor in building a skilled and stable workforce (2001). She discusses the need to standardize staff qualifications and develop a shared knowledge base—core competencies such as knowledge of child and youth development, health and safety issues, program development, and cultural competencies. She calls for more information on what the skills of school-age care practitioners should be and how they should be compensated for their work, as well as more data on what school-age care programs are doing in terms of their compensation policies and practices and how they recruit and retain practitioners. Increased compensation must be a part of any strategic plan to combat what Noonan calls a "negative return on investment" whereby the amount school-age care practitioners spend on higher education is usually higher than any associated increase in earning.

## Try This: Competencies and Compensation

Link pay to training. In our organization, we offer six full-day training modules per year. When our staff attend these training events, they get a dime raise in their hourly pay, which comes out to about $180 per year. We do this because we value learning, and the more competent they are, the more they deserve to be compensated.

## Training

The U.S. Department of Education (1998) states that staff should be provided with training and learning opportunities to prevent high rates of turnover. Research has shown that staff training is one of the most important components of high-quality programs and indicates the need to focus attention on the education of practitioners in order to reduce turnover (Vandenbergh & Locklear, 2000). Research has shown that paid time for preparation, paid time for training, formal mentoring, good in-house training, and commitment to staff training are effective strategies to reduce turnover (Chase, 2001).

Turnover is inversely related to the challenges of caring for children with behavior problems and job stress (Chase, 2001, p. 49). Good training on behavior management can help to relieve this stress. Other suggested training topics include how to work with children, how to negotiate, and how to adapt to the developmental needs of children. Training can give practitioners knowledge in enrichment and hands-on activities, greater expertise in academic support, knowledge in student assessment, and strategies for the different program components of academics, enrichment, and recreation.

Research findings strongly indicate a need for higher levels of training and professional preparation and enhancement of available resources to reduce turnover. One researcher's major findings included "a clear relationship between both training and program quality, and training and longevity in the field, which suggests that providing expanding training opportunities, especially for newer staff, may have positive implications for retention" (Morrow, 2000, p. 48). There was a statistically significant relationship between intent to leave and the amount of training respondents had received. Those who intended to leave had significantly less training (Morrow, 2000).

## Evaluation

After new staff have been well coached and trained, they need feedback. Ongoing, objective feedback is the most effective. Most organizations have a formal evaluation process as well. Staff should never be surprised by any feedback they receive during their evaluation. They should be receiving constant feedback and tips for how to improve (see the coaching section in chapter 3). When it is time for their formal evaluation, the staff member should be able to evaluate themselves just as well, if not better, than the supervisor. A good tool to help with this is the 360-degree evaluation.

This type of evaluation embraces our leadership philosophy that everyone, not just the supervisor, should take part in the job of evaluating each other. A 360-degree evaluation gives everyone in the program the opportunity to provide feedback to each employee. The evaluation tool consists of a self evaluation, a peer evaluation, a child evaluation, and a supervisor evaluation. The peer and child scores are combined so no individual stands out. The evaluation meeting then involves the employee discussing the self evaluation with the supervisor. The supervisor supports the employee with feedback from the other three parts of the tool. Usually, when done in this manner, the employee rates him or herself harder than the rest of the team. If a discrepancy develops, it is then discussed.

Retention, staff training, and evaluation are all ongoing processes that should take place continuously throughout each staff members' employment. While the process is the same, the method will change based on the situation and the needs of the employee.

## Full-Time Options

A profession with only part-time positions for most people is not a profession, it is an occupation. It is also a closed door for anyone who needs benefits, which includes most people with families. Most school-age programs operate for only a few hours each day. Many operate during the before and after school hours, and many operate only after school. Because of these hours of operation, many practitioners in school-age care can only be employed on a part-time basis.

In most cases part-time employees do not qualify for benefits such as health insurance. The Massachusetts Recruitment and Retention Project recommends providing full-time jobs as a strategy to reduce turnover in school-age care (NIOST, 2001a). Research has shown that offering full-time work and benefits is an effective strategy to reduce turnover, and that turnover is inversely related to offering health insurance (Chase, 2001). Research findings strongly indicate a need for collaborative efforts intended to create more full-time positions that include benefits in order to reduce turnover (Morrow, 2000).

## Try This: Full-Time Work

Restructure administrative positions to create more full-time positions. Many people leave our profession because they cannot get full-time employment. This is especially true in school-age child care. Since children are only with us part of the day, it is difficult finding enough work to justify a full-time schedule for our staff. In many organizations, part-time, entry-level staff work with the children. When they are great at their jobs they may get a promotion. They are promoted AWAY from the kids; promoted behind a desk. They are promoted to forty hours per week of administrative work. In order to create more full-time positions, we give those forty hours of work to three people who each continue to work twenty-seven hours per week with the children and thirteen hours doing administrative work. This keeps our best people doing what they do best—working with the kids—and also creates more full-time positions.

## Try This: Bye Bye

*Beat it.*
—*Michael Jackson*

The best way to lead great people is not to burden them with the people who are not performing. The moment you discover that you need to tightly manage

178

someone, you've made a hiring mistake. Guiding them and leading them is okay, but when you have to control them to get the behavior you expect it is time to say "bye bye." For every minute you allow a person to continue holding a seat on the bus when you know that person will not make it in the end, you're stealing a portion of his life, time he could be spending looking for a job in a better place where he could succeed (Collins, 2001).

Whenever possible, counsel the bad ones out of the job or out of the field entirely. It is better for both of you that they quit than be fired. If that is not possible, turn a bad hire into a good fire. The moment you know there is a problem, confront it and document it. We talked a lot about reducing turnover, but all turnover isn't bad. Some people aren't cut out for this work. This profession is supposed to be fun. Some people do this job for the HUGE paycheck, but stopped having fun a long time ago. We tell all new employees at their orientation that if this job stops being fun for them to GET OUT! This job is hard, sometimes difficult work. It isn't fun all of the time, but it should be fun a lot of the time. When people stop learning, stop growing, or stop laughing, it is time to get them off the bus. Yes, you can reduce turnover by getting the wrong people off the bus—systems in action.

## Try This: Exit Interviews

Conduct exit interviews. Do you know why people leave your organization? You can't fix possible retention problems if you don't understand the cause. Ask your people who quit why they are quitting. Ask them if they would recommend the job to others. Ask them if there is anything that you could have done to have kept them. Ask them these things after their last day of work so that you can be sure you get honest answers.

## Discussion Questions

1. How do you measure turnover?

2. What is the turnover rate of your organization? Do you track your turnover? Are you happy with your rate of turnover?

3. How much do you spend each year recruiting new staff?

4. How much time and money do you spend each year orienting new staff?

5. What have you noticed that happens to the quality of your program when good people leave? Do you notice changes in the children? Do you notice more mistakes?

## Helpful Resources

The Finance Project's Information Resource Center gives you easy access to a wealth of information on policies, programs, and financing strategies for initiatives striving to improve the lives of children, families and communities. There is a clearinghouse for developing, financing, and sustaining out-of-school time programs for children and youth.
www.financeproject.org

In this chapter we talked about many of the resources and materials we use at Children's Choice. Visit www.childrens-choice.org; from there you can find our resources using Facebook, Twitter, YouTube, our e-newsletter, and our blog!

*Get the Strategic Plan: Building a Skilled and Stable Out-of-School Time Workforce* at
www.niost.org/projects/stategic_plan_building_skilled.pdf

## Reference Notes

Campbell, N., Appelbaum, J., Martinson, K., & Martin, E. (2000). *Be all that we can be: Lessons from the military for improving our nations child care system.* Washington, DC: National Women's Law Center.

Collins, J. (2001). *Good to great: Why some companies make the leap and others don't.* New York: Harper Collins Publishers.

Chase, R. (2001). *Staff recruitment and retention in early childhood care and education and school-age care.* St Paul, MN: Wilder Research Center.

Helburn, S. (1995). *Cost, quality and child outcomes in child care centers.* Denver: University of Colorado at Denver.

Howes, C., Phillips, D., & Whitebook, M. (1992). Thresholds of quality: Implications for the social development of children in center-based child care. *Child Development* 63, 449–460.

Morrow, M. (2000). *Lifers and leavers: A comparison of school-age care practitioners who remain in the field and those who leave.* Portland, OR: Portland Community College and St Paul, MN: Concordia University.

Morgan, G. & Harvey, B. (2002). *New perspectives on compensation strategies for the out-of-school time workforce.* (Wellesley Centers for Women Working Paper Series Report No. CRW29). Wellesley, MA: Wellesley Centers for Women.

National Association of Elementary School Principals. (2001). *Principals and after-school programs: A survey of preK-8 principals.* Alexandria, VI: National Association of Elementary School Principals.

National Institute on Out-of-School Time. (2001a). *Massachusetts recruitment and retention project.* Wellesley, MA Retrieved October 28, 2002 from http://www.niost.org/mass_rr.html

National Institute on Out-of-School Time. (2001b). *Strategic planning: Building a skilled and stable workforce for after school programs.* Wellesley, MA Retrieved October 28, 2002 from http://www.niost.org/bssw.html

Noonan, A. (2001). From contrast to concrete: Issues in building a skilled and stable out-of-school time workforce. *After School Issues*, June 2001.

Roman, J. (Ed.). (1998). *The NSACA standards for quality school-age care.* Boston, MA: National School-Age Care Alliance.

Surr, W. (2001). Ready to Roll. *After School Issues,* March 2001.

U.S. Department of Education (1993). National study of before and after school programs. Washington D.C.: Office of Publishing and Planning.

U.S. Department of Education. (1998). *Safe and smart: Making after-school hours work for kids*. Washington, D.C.: U.S. Department of Justice, Office of Educational research and Improvement, Educational Resources Information center, U.S. Department of Justice.

Vandenbergh, B., & Locklear, E. (2000). *A profile of school-age care programs.* Raleigh, NC: North Carolina State University. Retrieved November 11, 2002 from http://www.joe.org/2000december/a1.html

Wexley, K., & Nemeroff, W. (1975). Effects of positive reinforcement and goal setting as methods of management development. *Journal of Applied Psychology,* 60, 446–450.

Whitebook, M. & Belm, D. (1999). *Taking on turnover: An action guide for child care center teachers and directors.* Washington D.C.: Center for the Child Care Workforce.

Whitebook, M., Howes, C., & Phillips, D. (1990). *Who cares? Child care teachers and the quality of care in America.* Final Report of the National Child Care Staffing Study. Washington, D.C.: Center for the Child Care Workforce.

YMCA of the USA. (2001). *Recruiting and retaining school-age care staff in today's challenging climate.* Chicago, IL: YMCA of the USA Program Store.

# Chapter 10: Making the Most of Meetings

*If we were meant to talk more than listen, we would have two mouths and one ear.*
—Mark Twain

*Bad meetings can take hours to put into minutes what can be accomplished in seconds.*
—Mike Ashcraft

## Introduction

We often hear people complain about having to go to meetings. We talk about them like going to the dentist. We've done it ourselves. It is a sad commentary on our experience with meetings. Imagine hearing a surgeon say, "I have to go to the operating room again, uggh." Imagine a symphony conductor saying, "I hate going to these concerts." As leaders, meetings are like our operating rooms, our concert stages. Meetings are the places where we get much of our work done. In order to get involvement in decision making, in order to share knowledge and information with our people, in order to hear the ideas and opinions of the people we work with, we sometimes need to sit down and meet. We could make decisions on our own. We could disseminate information through the use of memos, but that wouldn't be a high-involvement organization. Through magnificent meetings, we can get ownership, better results, more commitment, and accountability, but only if we do it right. This chapter will help you make the most of your meetings.

As a leader, meetings are a large part of your job. You will have meetings about many different topics and with many different people. Some meetings you hold will be with only a few people, while others may be quite large. In our organization:
- we have weekly leadership team meetings that last about two hours;
- every center has its own weekly staff meetings;
- we have design team meetings that write curriculum and plan for full-day summer day camps;
- we meet for orientations, staff training, and teambuilding retreats;
- we have quarterly board meetings;
- we have meetings with community groups that we partner with;
- we have monthly meetings with principals;

- we attend school faculty meetings;
- we have meetings with individual staff members for coaching and performance evaluations.

While meetings vary greatly in size and content, one thing remains constant. Effective leaders know how to balance task and relationship concerns in leading meetings (Yukl, 2002). Meetings help drive task-oriented behaviors.

Task-oriented behaviors assist systematic communication, evaluation, problem solving, and decision making. Task-oriented behaviors include developing an agenda, presenting a problem, soliciting information or ideas, keeping the discussion on track, reviewing and summarizing, suggesting procedures, assigning accountability, and ending the meeting. It is not sufficient for a leader to simply carry out task-oriented behaviors—a sense of timing is also essential. Summarizing too soon may stifle creativity. Allowing a discussion to go on too long may allow it to go off track or be unproductive and confusing (Yukl, 2002).

Group maintenance behaviors increase cohesiveness, improve interpersonal relations, aid conflict resolution, and satisfy the members' needs for respect and involvement. Group maintenance behaviors should be ongoing and designed to build teamwork and group cohesion, prevent apathy, manage conflict, and inhibit status struggles. Some examples of group maintenance behaviors include encouraging involvement by all members, preventing domination by any members, smoothing over conflict, suggesting compromises, enforcing ground rules of respect, win-win problem solving, expressing appreciation for participation, and using humor. Group maintenance functions are considered to be as important as the task-oriented functions, and the group shares responsibility for both types of functions. This style of leadership can improve the quality of the decisions and make members more satisfied with the group (Yukl, 2002).

Chelsea teaches child management courses at a local community college. Some of the best meetings I have attended have been led by the director of my department. First, she emails possible dates and times to all participants to get our availability a few weeks in advance. She then notifies the participants where and when the meeting will be held and gives us a brief agenda (sometimes she even requests our food preferences if it will be during the lunch hour). She reminds everyone about the meeting the day before with another email. She always starts the meeting on time, even if all the participants haven't arrived. She hands out a detailed agenda and starts each meeting with an overview of the information we need in order to accomplish the agenda items. She facilitates any questions or comments we may have on the information just presented, making sure we all stay on the topic.

She usually gives a break after the information part and then everyone chooses discussion groups based on the topic of their main interest. Each discussion group picks a leader to facilitate the conversation and records the work generated. After an adequate amount of time in our groups, each group presents the actions and decisions produced to the larger group. The notes from each group are given to the director to compile and disseminate to the participants a few days later. More comments and questions are allowed and then the action steps are summarized and agreed upon. The meeting is then adjourned on time.

Between meetings, the director holds each person accountable for the action they agreed to do so that by the next meeting, progress has happened. There are many reasons these meetings are successful. In this chapter, we will cover many techniques this director intentionally uses and provide many tips to help improve meetings you manage.

## Dialog
Learning Organizations are places for generative discussion and intensive action. Language functions as a tool for bonding, innovating, coordinating, and cooperating. People can speak from their hearts and connect with each other in the spirit of dialog—from the Greek dia + logos, moving through (Kofman & Senge, 1995).

Dialog is an essential element of organizational learning. Peter Senge identifies three conditions that are necessary for dialog to occur: all participants must suspend their assumptions; all participants must regard one another as colleagues; and there must be a facilitator who holds the context of the dialog (Senge, 1990).

When people talk and listen to each other, they create an alignment of purpose that produces incredible ability to invent new possibilities in conversation and bring about these possibilities in reality. There must be sufficient meeting time scheduled into people's professional calendars to step back from the day-to-day operations and reflect on what is happening in the organization. It is important for organizational leaders to understand that ideas can be developed best through dialog and discussion (Kline & Saunders, 1998). Through dialog, people can predict and solve problems, replace obsolete systems, and create new systems.

## Advance Preparation

*Your business clothes are naturally attracted to staining liquids. This attraction is strongest just before an important meeting.*
—Scott Adams

Preparation is the key to a successful meeting. Effective leaders visualize every piece of a meeting and organize them as if building a puzzle, ensuring that the meeting runs without a hitch and meets its goals. Effective leaders plant proper expectations by circulating the agenda in advance, previewing the meeting, and identifying what action is expected on each item. Details such as room size, seating arrangements, lighting, food, efficiencies, and comforts do make a difference. A meeting has two basic components, which must be carefully designed: the content and the administration (Yukl, 2002).

Skilled leaders of nonprofits put as much effort into meeting management as into any other operational task. Attention to detail and planning are essential. Participants want to contribute, to know what's going on, to network, and to learn. Meetings are tools for sharing information, generating ideas, hearing presentations, making decisions, planning for the future, and networking with colleagues. The substance of a meeting should reflect organizational values, goals, and mission and address concerns and challenges (Smith, Bucklin & Associates, Inc., 2000).

## Tips for Preparing for a Meeting

- Prepare based on the **purpose** of the meeting. What is the objective? What do you want to achieve? Can it be achieved through means other than a meeting? **Set goals** for your meeting. You can't present every aspect of the company's business at a one-hour meeting. So, decide the important, timely issues and spend the meeting time on them. Take into consideration the interests of the majority of the attendees as well.

Remember, you have other methods for communicating company information, too. It does not have to take place at the meeting.

- Prepare based on the **size** of the meeting. Keep it as small as possible to accomplish your objective. The larger the group the more complicated communication becomes. The more complex the subject, the fewer participants you need. Who will participate? On a small project team or task force, it will be easy to determine who should participate in meetings. However, in other situations, it's not always a clear choice. These questions provide a useful filter for choosing participants: Whose input do we need? Who's needed to make a decision?

- Prepare for **getting them there.** Once you know who you will invite, you must get them there—not always an easy task. If possible, call each person to tell them about the meeting, its overall purpose, and why their attendance is important. Follow-up your call with a meeting notice, including the purpose of the meeting, where it will be held and when, the list of participants, and whom to contact if they have questions. Send out a copy of the proposed agenda along with the meeting notice.

- Prepare based on the **time** of the meeting. Pick a time when participants are most likely to be on time and attentive and when disruptions are less likely to occur.

- Prepare based on the **length** of the meeting. An article in the *Wall Street Journal* several years ago stated that U.S. managers would save 80 percent of the time they waste in meetings if they did two things correctly. The first was to always have an agenda. The second was s**tart on time and end on time.** Waiting for participants who are late punishes those who are on time and encourages them to be late in the future. We've added that you need to allot each speaker the amount of time necessary to cover his or her topic. Hold them to their time limit—respectfully.

- Prepare an **agenda**. The agenda should clearly indicate the starting time, ending time, location, items to be covered, and what advance preparation participants need to do. Place the most important items first on the agenda. Next to each major topic, include the type of action needed, the type of output expected (decision, vote, or action assigned to someone). Formulate the agenda carefully. Identify the needs and interests of the majority of the participants. Start with good news that will set a positive tone. For recurring meetings, vary the order of the speakers on the agenda. Novelty drives attention. You don't want people bored by sameness. Design the agenda so that participants get involved early by having something for them to do right away and so they come on time. Don't overly design meetings; be willing to adapt the meeting agenda if members are making progress in the planning process. Think about how you label an event, so people come in with that mindset; it may pay to have a short dialog around the label to develop a common mindset among attendees, particularly if they include representatives from various cultures. Preparing an agenda also helps participants know what they should be talking about and keeps the conversation focused. Anybody can ask if the conversation is still on-topic. If the meeting is off-course, don't wait for the leader to notice. Keeping a meeting focused is everyone's job! Meeting management tends to be a set of skills often overlooked by leaders and managers. Keep in mind that meetings are very expensive activities when one considers the cost of labor for the meeting and how much can or cannot get done in them. The end of this chapter gives some helpful tips on how to keep a meeting on track.

- Prepare **the environment**. Organize the physical environment so people are attentive to the meeting content. Plan for seating—where will the leader of the meeting sit? No one should sit behind or to the side of your speakers. Make sure there are seats for all attendees, and if taking notes is required, there is a surface to write on. Make sure visuals are visible and that people can hear. You may need to use a microphone. You can pass props or samples around the room for viewing. Minimize distractions and interruptions. Plan enough space for all participants to sit and spread out their things. Keep the temperature on the chilly side.

- Prepare for **biology**. Provide food and water. Never underestimate the power of food at a meeting. Food relaxes the atmosphere, helps make people feel comfortable, helps people sustain positive energy levels and builds the camaraderie of the team. Ensure you meet the diverse needs of your group with the food you serve. As an example, offer fruit and yogurt in addition to donuts. Offer vegetarian and kosher hot dogs with the regular franks.

## Try This: Getting to Know You

Do "get-to-know-you" activities. Trust is important in a team. Trust is built when we truly get to know each other. If you have a team that is new or has some new members on it, they may need for this to happen. If your meetings are all about the business of the business, this happens slowly. You can jump start the process by facilitating some "get to know you" conversations. We sometimes take a few minutes at the beginning of a meeting to ask questions such as, "Where did you grow up? Who did you spend time with growing up? What are your pet peeves? When someone has a problem with you, how do you want them to tell you?"

## Tips for Facilitating Discussions

- **Plant proper expectations.** Circulate an agenda, preview the meeting, and identify what action is expected on each item.
- **Keep the energy level high**. Start your meetings, presentations, and training sessions with an icebreaker or warm-up activity. In a large meeting or a short meeting, the icebreaker can be a single question that gets people thinking and talking with their neighbor. As an example, ask a question that causes people to raise their hands. The length of the ice-breaker depends on the length of your meeting, so plan wisely. Use animated body language. Move around. Use energizing music before the meeting. Keep the meeting moving at a fast pace. Challenge the participants with questions.
- **Ask provocative, open-ended questions.** Ask questions that induce a free flow of information. Ask probing questions that keep people talking.
- **Avoid excessive negativism**. Don't "fire hose" new ideas or opinions of participants—that will destroy creativity and lead to poor decision making. Fire hosing happens when others quickly and forcibly criticize an idea (in much the same way a firefighter's hose puts out a house fire). Acknowledge people for participating. Set up ground rules for giving constructive criticism.
- **Use brainstorming.** Brainstorming is a way to inspire creativity and generate ideas. It is structured thinking; a wide open, anything is possible, free flow of ideas; an analytical technique; a starting place when looking for ideas. The objective of brainstorming is to gather large quantities of creative ideas as quickly as possible. The generation of creative

ideas requires a particular environment—one that is non-linear, non-judgmental and quick-paced. Brainstorming meets these requirements by encouraging participants to suggest many ideas, without limiting them with considerations of reasonableness, accuracy, practicality, or cost.

To encourage participation from the entire group, it is imperative that there be no initial judgment on or discussion of any of the ideas that are generated. Not only does judgment hinder the association or thought process it also slows down the exercise and discourages participation

- **General Rules for Brainstorming**
  - Decide on your limits. The limits can be on the duration of the brainstorming session, the number of ideas you want to collect, or to stop at the first (or second or third) natural lull in the flow of ideas.
  - Generate excitement and enthusiasm. People can only be creative when they are in a positive frame of mind. Remind the participants of the benefits of coming up with one or more break-through concepts and sell them on it. Set the tone with your actions and voice. Radiate positive, up-beat feelings. Let them see your enthusiasm for the process and for the possibilities that WILL come out of the exercise.

    Encourage creativity. Anything goes! Remind participants that this is a non-linear process and one of its objectives is the generation of innovative ideas. Innovative ideas are not found by sticking to the norm.
  - Do not allow participants to comment on, discuss, or judge any of the points raised. The room is to be quiet except for the ideas. Record everything that is said and encourage the flow of ideas.
  - Keep the pace moving. This fosters the feeling of excitement and enthusiasm. You may have to be very encouraging initially and you may have to use many filler words such as: "Give me more who has some other ideas say whatever you are thinking right now."
  - Go for quantity. The greater the number of ideas recorded the better.

## Creative Decision Making

Participation is paramount to good decision making. Receiving a report on operations may be important, but debating a course of action, being heard, and making a difference is much more fulfilling (Smith, Bucklin & Associates, Inc., 2000). Effective leaders encourage and facilitate participation by all members. Do not allow dominant members to force through their own agendas. Do not assume that silent members are in agreement—silence may indicate dissent. Each member should be encouraged to contribute ideas and concerns and discouraged from dominating the discussion using social pressure tactics to intimidate people who disagree (Yukl, 2002).

Two useful techniques for creating a supportive climate for idea generation are positive restatement and idea building. Positive restatement requires group members to restate another member's idea and find something worthwhile about it before saying anything critical. With idea building, a member who points out a deficiency or limitation of another's idea is required to propose a way to correct the deficiency or overcome the drawback (Yukl, 2002).

## Try This: Mine for Conflict

In the book *Death by Meeting*, Lencioni (2004) compares meetings to various forms of entertainment. One of the things that makes a movie interesting is conflict; it is what keeps us on the edge of our seats. Anxiety increases when there is conflict within a group trying to resolve a situation. This anxiety can make a leader uncomfortable, so sometimes he "bails out" by changing the subject or smoothing things over. When conflict arises he hides it, buries it, or ignores it. When that happens a pattern gets established so that people talk around difficult issues, retiring to their offices without a clear sense of what decisions were made or what they should do next.

A good leader of a meeting can look for areas in which group members have differing opinions and dig them up—psychiatrists call it mining for conflict. It can lead to heated, passionate, unfiltered, messy, and provocative discussions, but it is important to get all of the issues out on the table. Only when that happens can great informed decisions be made. Avoiding conflict can be much more dangerous than mining for it.

## Tips for Success

- **Diversify your presentation methods.** If every speaker talks to the audience in lecture format, even interested heads soon nod. Ask people to talk in small groups. Use audio-visual materials such as overheads, PowerPoint presentations, and pictures. If you're talking about a new program idea, show your employees examples. Pass around positive customer surveys and comment cards.

- **Invite guest speakers** for audience participation and excitement. Your customers have lots to say to your workforce about their needs and quality requirements. Speakers from organizations your employees support financially are dynamite.

- **Encourage questions to get a dialog going.** Ask people to write down their questions in advance of the meeting and during the meeting. Allow time for questions directed to each speaker as you go. If you can't answer the question immediately and correctly, tell the people you'll get back with them when you have the correct answer. If questions exceed time, schedule a meeting on the topic.

- In a large meeting, an often-overlooked, but very important, successful meeting tactic is to ask each speaker to **repeat out loud every question** he or she is asked. The person asking the question then knows the speaker understood the question. Other people attending the meeting can hear and know the question, too, not just surmise the question—perhaps incorrectly—from the speaker's response.

- Once the meeting has concluded, arrange for the recorder's notes to be posted or distributed to all participants. **Post-meeting communication** provides form and closure both to participants' contributions and their social needs. A lack of clarity in meeting notes can drag unfinished business to the forefront of your next meeting and unnecessarily slow the group's progress towards its long-range goals. Tending to both the content and process aspects of your meetings will go a long way toward making them more effective and productive.

## Tips for Competing Conversations

*I have left orders to be awakened at any time in case of national emergency, even if I'm in a cabinet meeting.*
*—Ronald Reagan*

Off-topic conversations between two or more group members waste time, inhibit group progress, and limit the contributions of individuals to the team meeting as a whole. They are distracting for meeting participants who want to participate in all interactions. They make for boring meetings for anyone not directly involved in the side conversation.

- **Use non-verbal communication.** Look steadily at the participants for a moment. Raise your eyebrows while looking or wave to the participants. Stop the person who has the floor for a minute while the other participants rejoin the group.
- **Ask a question.** Call on one of the group members participating in the competing conversation. With a brief summary of the discussion occurring in the meeting as a whole, ask for his opinion. Ask him to share his ideas with the rest of the people in the meeting. Say, "I believe we'd all be interested in your thoughts on this issue, John."
- **Verbally intervene.** Directly ask the group members participating in the competing conversation to rejoin the group discussion, without using sarcasm or anger. Say, "I'm afraid we're missing good ideas when everyone is talking at once. I know I can't keep track of all these thoughts."
- **Establish group ownership.** Leaders can make a spontaneous break-out session public by saying: "This discussion appears to involve only a few people. Is it something that can be resolved rapidly or is there another way to handle this? What does the group want to do?"
- **Establish a group signal.** The group signal reminds participants to hold one discussion at a time. One that works effectively is to make a non-verbal time out sign (like a sports referee) followed by holding up one index finger to indicate "one meeting." If this signal is set up in advance, it can add humor to a typically uncomfortable situation.

## Tips for Not Going Off-Topic

Meetings don't go off-topic, people do. It usually takes at least two people adrift to take the meeting off-course. That means you don't have to be an expert on meetings to help. You just have to notice when certain things show up in a meeting's conversations.

- **Topic drift.** Any topic that can attract comments irrelevant to the meeting agenda or objective. Juicy as they are, such comments seduce one or more participants. If pursued—well, you've been there—conversation diverges farther. Topic drift (sometimes called "being in the weeds") can be more fun and interesting than the meeting's objective, but can only be briefly tolerated if the group is to achieve its original purpose.

- **What to do.** For a minor diversion, treat the occurrence lightly: "Okay, let's come back and focus on the problem we need to solve..." When participants have been seriously diverted, say: "This discussion appears to be veering into areas outside the scope of this meeting. Can we table it or do we need to add it to the agenda?"

- **Great leader tip.** When you suspect a conversation has abandoned the objective or agenda of the meeting, verify your assessment by calling for a clarity check (sometimes called a process check). Get the group's attention and then say: "Excuse me, I'm not clear that this conversation is on-topic. I'd like to check to see if it's important to pursue now." If it's not important, other participants will confirm your assessment and those engaged in the conversation can be asked to continue off-line.

- **Breaking time agreements.** Time agreements are typically broken in two ways: The start and end times of the meeting aren't honored, or the budgeted time for a given agenda item isn't honored. Both problems can prevent the meeting from reaching its objective and cause participants to feel frustrated by the process.

- **What to do.** Call for a realistic agreement: "I notice that we don't heed our stated start and end times, which causes a bind for me. Could we make a new agreement that reflects our true intentions and practice?" Announce it when agenda items run over budgeted time: "We have spent more time on this item than intended. What does the group want to do?" Of course, if you assign more time, you'll need to reallocate the entire meeting's time budget at this point.

## Ending the Meeting

*When the outcome of a meeting is to have another meeting, it has been a lousy meeting.*
—Herbert Hoover

People tend to remember what comes last in a meeting. The closing is important. Summarizing can be used to end a meeting to ensure that everyone has a clear overview of what took place or what action is now required. It is an invaluable skill for a meeting leader. Summarizing requires active listening. You have to state concisely what was said in an impartial way and end with a clear statement about what is expected to happen next. It takes practice to summarize well, but it is a skill well worth developing (McNamara, 2004).

Leave five to ten minutes at the end of the meeting for evaluation; don't skip this portion of the meeting. Have each member fill out a questionnaire or quickly rank the meeting from one to five with a silent show of raised fingers. Have the chief executive rank the meeting last. Always end meetings on time and attempt to end on a positive note. At the end of a meeting, review actions and assignments, and set the time for the next meeting and ask each person if they can make it or not (to get their commitment). Clarify that meeting minutes and/or actions will be reported back to members in at most a week. This helps to keep momentum going (McNamara, 2004).

Summarizing can be used to end a topic, to end a discussion, to limit the need for discussion, and at the end of a meeting to ensure that everyone has a clear overview of what took place or what action is now required. It is an invaluable skill. Summarizing requires active listening. You have to state concisely what was said in an impartial way and end with a clear statement about what is expected to happen next. It takes practice to summarize well, but it is a skill well worth developing.

## Try This: ConsensoGrams

Use a "ConsensoGram" when you are trying to solve a problem or make a decision as a group, and you want to provide a non-threatening way of getting everyone's opinion. Write some of the options or potential solutions on flip charts and put them up on the walls around the room. Have participants "vote" by putting a sticky note on their choice or on their "top three" choices. You can quickly look around the room and get a sense of the group's opinions.

## Discussion Questions

1. What meetings do you attend on a regular basis? How would you characterize those meetings?

2. What are some elements of a great meeting? Have you ever left a meeting thinking that it was a great use of your time? What happened there to make it magnificent?

3. If you were in charge of the meetings you attend, how would you change them?

## Helpful Resources

*Death by Meeting* by Patrick Lencioni (2004). San Francisco, CA: Jossey-Bass.

Get information on how to make meetings more effective, and find some brief tips on increasing effectiveness, motivation, involvement, participation, and after-meeting results at
www.toolpack.com/meetings.html

## Reference Notes

Kofman, F., Senge, P. M. (1995). Communities of commitment: The heart of learning organizations. In S. Chawla & J. Renesch (Eds.), *Learning Organizations* (p. 11–45). Portland, OR: Productivity Press.

Kline, P., & Saunders, B. (1998). *Ten steps to a learning organization*. Arlington, VA: Great Ocean Publishers.

McNamara, C. (2004). *Basic guide to conducting effective meetings*. Retrieved July 7, 2004, from http://humanresources.about.com

Senge, P. M. (1990). *The fifth discipline: The art and practice of the learning organization*. New York, NY: Doubleday.

Smith, Bucklin & Associates, Inc. (2000). *The complete guide to nonprofit management.* New York: John Wiley and Sons, Inc.

Yukl, G. (2002). *Leadership in organizations.* Upper Saddle River, NJ: Prentice Hall.

# Part V: The End

# Chapter 11: Wrapping it Up

*Without play—without the child that still lives in all of us—we will always be incomplete. And not only physically, but creatively, intellectually, and spiritually as well.*
*—George Sheehan*

*Hey everybody, let's have some fun. You only live once and when you're dead you're done. So let the good times roll!*
*—B. B. King*

## Introduction

Leadership is challenging. You need a positive attitude and ability to laugh at yourself and find fun in everything you do. Bad things happen, sure; but you can find the pony in the manure pile, promote the positive, find the good, and help others to see it also. Playing and promoting the positive build the curiosity and creativity needed to become a great leader. You can't become a great leader, heck, you can't do any of the things discussed in this book without this. Playing, learning, and living are essential for leadership, for coping, and for managing stress.

## Story Time: Sharpen the Saw

*He that would perfect his work must first sharpen his tools.*
*—Confucius*

"Sharpen the Saw" is the seventh of Stephen Covey's *Habits of Highly Effective People*. He introduces the habit with the following metaphor.

"Suppose you were to come upon someone in the woods working feverishly to saw down a tree."

"What are you doing?" you ask.

"Can't you see?" comes the impatient reply. "I'm sawing down this tree."

"You look exhausted!" you exclaim. "How long have you been at it?"

"Over five hours," he returns, "and I'm beat! This is hard work."

"Well why don't you take a break for a few minutes and sharpen that saw?" you inquire. "I'm sure it would go a lot faster."

"I don't have time to sharpen the saw," the man says emphatically. "I'm too busy sawing!" (2004, p. 287).

It is important to sharpen your personal and professional saws. Sharpening the saw can include opportunities for spiritual, physical, emotional, and intellectual growth. It can include time for relaxation and reflection. It can include time for learning and reading for pleasure. You can only be a great leader if you take the time to sharpen your saw. Take time to have some fun. Take time to play. You deserve it!

## Story Time: Two Seeds

It was springtime, and a lovely young woman planted her garden. Two seeds ended up lying in the ground next to each other. The first seed said to the second one: "Think of how fun this will be! We will let our roots grow deep down into the soil, and when they are strong we will burst from the ground and become beautiful flowers for the entire world to see and admire!"

The second seed heard this, but was worried. "That sounds nice," he said, "but isn't the ground too cold? I'm frightened to try to put my roots into it. And what if something goes wrong and I don't turn out very pretty? And what if the lovely lady doesn't like me? I'm scared of not succeeding!"

The first seed, however, was not about to be stopped. He pushed his roots down into the ground and immediately began to grow. When they were strong enough he burst from the ground and soon became a beautiful flower. The lovely young woman tended carefully to him and proudly showed him to all her friends. He was very happy. "Come on," he said to his friend every day, "it's wonderful and warm up here in the sunshine!"

The second seed was quite impressed with what the first seed had become. However, even though he could see what was possible, he was still very scared. He tentatively pushed one of his roots into the ground. "Ouch," he said. "This ground is still much too cold for me! I don't like it. I think I'll just stay inside my shell where I'm comfortable. Besides, I'm quite safe inside my own shell. I'll become a flower later. There's plenty of time." Nothing the first seed could say would change his mind.

One day, when the young woman was away, a very hungry bird flew in the garden. It scratched at the ground looking for seeds to eat. The second seed, still lying inside its shell, was terrified of what would happen if he was found. But this was his lucky day, and the bird did not find him. Finally it flew away.

When the bird was gone, the second seed breathed a sigh of relief. But he also had come to a decision. While hiding inside his shell he had realized that perhaps he had been wrong in thinking that there was always plenty of time to become a flower. Perhaps, he thought, no one should take for granted that there will be plenty of time to explore their hopes and dreams. Perhaps, sometimes, everyone needs to simply take a chance and reach for a goal. So that's exactly what he did. Without another word, he pushed his roots out into the ground and quickly grew into a beautiful flower.

## Story Time: Making the Best of It

Chelsea's ninety-four-year-old grandmother has unintentionally taught her a valuable lesson about life. She is someone who has spent her entire life going through the motions. She has had some really great times and some really tragic times. Apparently, she had never understood that while she may not have had control over the things that have happened to her, she did have control over the way she felt and dealt with the situations. She has never been a person to make the best of it. Now that she is living in an assisted living home, she feels she is in hell. While her room is nice and her care is good, she doesn't like to eat in the dining room. Because of this one discomfort, she is unable to make the best of it. No matter how much we try to explain that she has the power to change her attitude about this place, she remains miserable. Because of her experience, I realize that making the best of it in every situation is vital to living a happy life—especially if I get to make it to ninety-four.

Children are not the only ones who benefit from unstructured downtime—time to do whatever their heart desires. Leaders also need to play, for their health, their minds, and their very sanity. When you take time to do something you love, levels of dopamine and serotonin rise in your body, which makes you feel calm and pleasant. Take time to connect with your family and friends. Take time to make new friends. Read, reflect inwardly, pray, and play! Learn a new skill or hone an old one. Relax and de-stress. Take time to do something creative.

"You feel happier, healthier, and more fulfilled when you can do things that provide the kind of satisfaction you're looking for," says Howard E.A. Tinsley, Ph.D., professor emeritus of psychology at Southern Illinois University. "Over the long term, the ability to do these kinds of things leads to a greater level of physical and mental health, and to a higher quality of life."

Playtime is also essential to help adults relieve stress, says Blair Justice, Ph.D., professor of psychology at the University of Texas School of Public Health. "You don't have time to make yourself sick," he says. "However, when adults become overly stressed and don't take time for leisure, they do just that. Too much stress leads to increases in chemicals such as cortisol and norepinephrine, which can disrupt the immune system and cause you to feel edgy and hostile. Studies have also found a link between high levels of these chemicals and heart disease."

You can't be a great leader if you don't take the time to play!

## Story Time: Madison's Funny Wave

A couple of years ago we were in California for a speaking engagement. We arrived a couple of days early for some family play time. We drove from New Mexico and when we arrived we went straight to the beach, took off our shoes, and dipped our tootsies in the Pacific. Our daughter, Madison, and Mike were playing with the incoming waves. When the tide went out, we would chase it into the ocean. Then, when the wave would come in we would "back pedal," letting the wave chase us, being careful not to get our pants wet, being careful not to turn our backs on the ocean.

It was kind of chilly, and Madison was wearing a pair of sweats. One time we weren't quite careful enough and Madi got her sweats a little wet. Chelsea had the thought, "Oops I should have rolled the cuff of her pant legs up, so they didn't get wet. Oh, well."

A few moments later, Madison was getting accustomed to the ocean and she let her guard down. She chased the wave into the ocean, and then she turned her back on the Pacific. The next wave was a biggie! Chelsea and I were watching what was about to happen, powerless to prevent it. The wave overtook her and smacked her down into the sand. Mike was a little scared and rushed to pick her up. She was soaked head to toe. There was sand in her hair and salt water and snot were running down her face. She was crying. I looked back at Mommy to show her that I had rescued our baby girl and she was laughing! She had just had the thought that she should have rolled her pant cuffs up and now Madison was soaked. That struck her as funny, so she was laughing.

I didn't know why she was laughing, but it was contagious. I started laughing too! Madison was still crying, and she did not like the fact that we were laughing. As we tried to get our laughing under control, Mommy explained why she had started laughing. Madison was too wet and upset to understand. We took her to the car and got her into some dry clothes, and Chelsea again tried to explain that we were not laughing AT her. She tried to explain what had struck her as funny. Chelsea asked, "Now do you see why I thought it was funny?" Madison replied, "It might be funny if I wasn't so c...c...co...cold." After we got her all dry and warm she agreed that she could see the humor in the situation, but we still didn't get much of a smile from her.

A couple of days later, some of our colleagues arrived at the conference. We picked them up at the airport. Madison was in the back of the van with them. We overheard her saying, "Hey do you guys want to hear a funny story about something that happened to me?" Then she told her "funny" wave story.

The moral of this story is that humor and the ability to laugh at ourselves is a powerful coping strategy. Learning to laugh at ourselves when we get knocked down can help us bounce back. It is important to deal with the negative stuff, dry off, and get warm, but after that, playfulness and humor can help us handle negative situations. Playfulness creates resiliency!

## Conclusion

*Draw a crazy picture, Write a nutty poem, Sing a mumble-gumble song, Whistle through a comb. Do a loony-goony dance, 'Cross the kitchen floor, Put something silly in the world that ain't been there before.*
—Shel Silverstein

*The supreme accomplishment is to blur the line between work and play.*
—Arnold Toynbee

The adults in our society are very busy and seem to want children to be just as busy. It is no wonder children are suffering from the same stress-related illnesses as busy adults. The loss of childhood is a syndrome described by David Elkind in *The Hurried Child* (1988) and *Ties that Stress* (1998), and by Neil Postman in *The Disappearance of Childhood* (1994). As practitioners in the child care and youth development field we understand the importance of play in the learning lives of children. The message here is that as leaders, we need to understand that play is just as important for our employees and ourselves. In the child care and youth development field, none of us are paid what we are worth. The playfulness and the laughter that comes with working in this field are part of our compensation package. It feeds our souls. Don't apologize for the fact that we get to play in this profession. Embrace it!

*Goodnight, sweetheart, well it's time to go. I hate to leave you, but I really must say, goodnight, sweetheart, goodnight.*
—The Spaniels

*Na na na na, na na na na, hey hey-ey, goodbye!*
—Steam

## About the Authors

Mike and Chelsea have been active in the child and youth development field since 1989. They currently live in the small mountain community of Cedar Grove, New Mexico, with their two wonderful daughters, Madison and Adeline. Mike and Chelsea met while working at a YMCA that ran a summer day camp and school-age child care program. Together they have more than forty years of experience working with children and youth. They successfully managed a number of camps and afterschool programs, and Chelsea directed a corporate child care center for a number of years.

Mike and Chelsea are co-founders and CEOs of Children's Choice Child Care Services in Albuquerque, New Mexico. Children's Choice provides school-age child care and development programs as well as staff training and technical assistance all across the country. Mike taught courses in brain-based teaching and middle childhood development for Concordia University. Mike is a former President of both the NM School-Age Care Alliance and the NM Association for the Education of Young Children. Chelsea developed and teaches the Afterschool Professional Certification course for Central New Mexico College, where she also teaches courses in leadership, child care management, early childhood guidance, and teaching strategies. Mike is the author of *Best Practices: Guidelines for School-Age Programs and the Best Practices Workbook.*

They frequently teach workshops, seminars, and keynotes. They have presented at many national conferences. They provide training in the areas of Afterschool Programming, Behavior Management, Child Development, Brain Development, Social Skills, Customer Service, Leadership, and a course on Brain-Compatible Staff Training.

For a complete list of topics and descriptions and FREE handouts, visit www.childrens-choice.org. They can be reached at ashcraft@childrens-choice.org.

Typical audiences include:
- Afterschool Program Staff
- Camp Staff
- Early Childhood Educators
- Elementary Educators
- Adult Educators, Staff Trainers, and College Instructors